A
Pocket Guide
of
Movement Activities
for the
Elementary School

illustrations by RUE WISE

MARJORIE LATCHAW   *University of California, Los Angeles*

A
Pocket Guide
of
Movement Activities
for the
Elementary School

SECOND EDITION

PRENTICE-HALL, INC. Englewood Cliffs, New Jersey

13-684852-4

Library of Congress Catalog Card Number 70-102134

Printed in the United States of America

Current printing (last digit)

10 9 8 7 6 5 4 3 2 1

PRENTICE-HALL INTERNATIONAL, INC., London
PRENTICE-HALL OF AUSTRALIA, PTY. LTD., Sydney
PRENTICE-HALL OF CANADA, LTD., Toronto
PRENTICE-HALL OF INDIA PRIVATE LTD., New Delhi

INTRODUCTION

The promise of the twenty-first century and our expectations, based upon the predictions of a brilliant technology that will cause drastic changes in our daily lives, give rise to the problem of today's education: What kind of person is needed for the "new world" and how can the schools provide best for his learning? The challenge of changing social institutions, particularly the balance between the "haves"

has made necessary new approaches to old problems, not only in our own country but everywhere.

New approaches may not necessarily demand a completely new curriculum. Rather, they may direct us to look again at the goals and tasks of the school in preparing an individual for a productive and satisfying life in a changing world. It has been said that management and maintenance are more likely to determine educational programs than the needs of the child. This is particularly true in physical education, where the program is likely to be determined by available facilities, equipment, or class size, rather than by needs of children.

This second edition of the *Pocket Guide of Games and Rhythms for the Elementary School* is focused on children's development, both conceptual and biological, through the medium of movement. Games and other movement activities may be used for many purposes. The child may learn how better to control his environment through experiencing many types of movement. He may learn how to use movement for the development of strength, endurance, flexibility, coordination, skill in performance and other biologi-

Introduction   1

cal factors. He may discover movement as a satisfying means of expression and communication. Two large conceptual areas in children's learning are those of understanding human movement and understanding biological development. Having many movement opportunities during childhood may help the child acquire such understanding, particularly if the teacher structures movement activities for this purpose.

This second edition of the *Pocket Guide* is a collection of *movement activities* using a variety of gross movement skills, a *Pocket Guide of Movement Activities for the Elementary School.* These activities are organized under traditional headings to facilitate their use by the teacher. Activities under each major area are presented in order from simple to complex and are identified by grade level from kindergarten through grade 6. The description of each activity includes (1) brief, concise directions for performing the activity, (2) a brief statement of the behavioral goal to be achieved, (3) an illustration of the activity, and (4) an evaluative check list based upon criteria relating to concepts in human movement and biologic development, and the growth and development of children in our democratic American culture.

Although grade levels are designated for most of the activities, many of the activities are challenging to children of all ages and should be selected freely to help children reach specific behavioral goals or to develop specific skills and concepts. Many familiar activities reappear in this edition, some in space-age garb to capture the interests of our space-age children. Teachers and children are encouraged to modify and expand these materials, adapting activities to varying groups of children and originating new activities as they are needed to help children achieve their goals.

A recommended group size is suggested for each activity, but this may be varied according to the situation. Groups that are too large find it difficult to function effectively. If children are to learn how to solve their problems, to grow in self-reliance, and to get along with each other, situations must be provided in which these experiences may be put into action, where each voice may be heard, where each opinion may be considered, and where each player may have his turn at a favored position.

The following guidelines related to human movement, biologic development, and cultural develop-

apply the evaluative materials at the end of each activity.

HUMAN MOVEMENT

1. Human movement takes place in the joints of the body and is caused by muscles pulling on bones, resulting in a change of position of a body member or of the body as a whole.

2. The basic movements of the body are bending, stretching, and twisting. All body movements are combinations of these three movements and include the skills of locomotion such as running, jumping, swimming, and the skills of overcoming inertia of external objects such as striking, catching, throwing.

3. Physical education includes the study and performance of human movement skills that use all or most of the body, moving in large spatial areas. *Movement skill* means competence in the performance of a particular movement pattern, such as batting a ball or serving a volleyball.

4. In giving impetus to an external object (striking, throwing, pushing, and the like) the center of mass of the body should be moving in the direction of the goal. Widening the base of support by taking a stride position in the desired direction will help one to accomplish this.

(catching, recovering from a shove, and the like), or is receiving impetus from oneself, as in landing from a jump or fall, the center of mass moves in the direction of the force and gradually diminishes the force. This is called "giving" with the ball in catching, or landing with "rubber legs." Lowering the center of gravity and widening the base of support by bending the knees and spreading the feet also helps one to maintain balance.

6. Stability and balance can be improved by: (1) increasing the frictional resistance between the supporting surface and the body, as when wearing rubber-soled shoes on clean floors; (2) placing the center of mass over the base of support by assuming the correct body position; (3) lowering the center of gravity by bending the knees; (4) widening the base of support by spreading the feet apart.

7. The longer the lever, the greater the speed at the end of the lever. Implements used in sports, such as baseball bats and tennis rackets, extend the reach and increase the amount of force that can be applied to the ball due to the greater speed at the end of the extended levers.

8. The summation of forces for effective movement is dependent upon a sequential contribution of the various levers of the body. For example, just before the batter begins to swing the bat he should start his center of mass moving in the direction of the swing. If the center of mass is permitted to come to rest before the swing starts, any contribution that the movement could make to the summation of

forces is eliminated and the power of the swing is reduced. Starting the swing too soon and slowing it down to correct the timing to strike a ball also reduces the ultimate power of the swing.

9. To change the direction of movement of the body, the weight must be shifted to the foot that is away from the given direction of movement. For example, a child who wishes to move rapidly to the right must first bend both knees slightly, then push against the ball of the right foot, thus shifting the center of gravity of his body toward the left foot. As the center of gravity moves over the base of support provided by the left foot, the right foot can be lifted from the ground and the initial step in the new direction can be taken. The more rapid the change, the lower the center of gravity is placed over the base of support to provide a stronger push-off as the new step is being taken.

BIOLOGIC DEVELOPMENT

1. Strength is the ability of the organism to mobilize force in an effort to overcome resistance. Strength may be developed only if the muscle is overloaded, which means that the muscle does more work in each succeeding period of exercise.

2. Overloading may be accomplished through (1) increasing the intensity of the exercise (usually by increasing the work load), (2) increasing the duration of the exercise, adding repetitions during successive activity periods, and (3) increasing the rate at which an individual exercises (reducing the amount of time allowed for each exercise).

3. Endurance is the capacity of the body to withstand the cumulative effects of stress accompanying muscular work. Conditions that affect endurance are muscular, circulo-respiratory, psychological, and mechanical, assuming that all conditions for healthy growth and development are present.

4. Muscles with the greatest strength have the greatest endurance, and stronger muscles utilize fewer fibers for a given amount of work than do weaker muscles. Thus, the development and maintenance of muscular strength is an important factor in the development and maintenance of endurance.

5. The circulo-respiratory aspect of endurance is the ability of the organism to extract and use oxygen, and it can be developed by a progressive increase in levels of activity with a resultant increased demand upon the circulatory and respiratory systems. As the intensity of endurance-type activities, such as running, progressively increases over a period of years, the organism steadily improves in its ability to withstand the cumulative stresses of prolonged work.

6. The psychological aspect of endurance is related to the individual's willingness to accept the discomfort of strenuous effort. This acceptance level improves with training.

7. Improved mechanical efficiency of movement will bring about an improved level of skill performance and the fewer

less the energy demands, thus permitting the individual to endure for a longer period of time for the same energy cost.

8. Flexibility is described by the range of motion in the various joints of the body. Each joint has limits placed upon it by (1) joint structure, (2) condition of the ligaments, (3) muscle adaptation, and (4) injury. Since the structure of the joint is permanent, flexibility may be increased through alteration of the range of motion by forced stretching of the musculature that is limiting the movement. One should stretch in a slow, controlled manner without losing momentum, in order to safeguard against injury, and only after an adequate warm-up. Endurance exercises are recommended as warm-up exercises before stretching.

9. There should be a balance of strength in the musculature on opposite sides of a joint. Since all muscles exert force by pulling, the stronger muscle could cause the weaker muscle to adapt to a habitually lengthened position, resulting in changes in flexibility of the joint. Consistent changes involving a number of joints can result in movement difficulties.

SOCIAL DEVELOPMENT

1. In a democratic society the worth and dignity of the individual is primary, and the human personality represents the ultimate value. Each individual must feel his own worth and respect the worth of others.

himself and others.

3. The individual must be inquiring and experimental. He must be capable of contributing to and participating in a changing world.

4. The individual must be able to live in voluntary group life. He must participate cooperatively with others in working for the common good.

5. The individual must be able to make decisions based upon the facts and values of a democratic society.

Resources for further study, which give a more comprehensive treatment to the theory and science of human movement applicable to the school physical education program, are as follows.

BROWN, CAMILLE and ROSALIND CASSIDY, *Theory in Physical Education* (Philadelphia: Lea & Fabiger, 1963).

ESPENSCHADE, ANNA S., and HELEN M. ECKERT, *Motor Development* (Columbus, Ohio: Charles E. Merrill Books, Inc., 1967).

HACKETT, LAYNE C. and ROBERT G. JENSON, *A Guide to Movement Exploration* (Palo Alto Calif.: Peek Publications, 1967).

LATCHAW, MARJORIE, and GLEN H. EGSTROM, *Human Movement With Concepts Applied to Children's Movement Activities* (Englewood Cliffs, N. J.: Prentice-Hall, Inc., 1969).

METHENY, ELEANOR, *Movement and Meaning* (New York: McGraw-Hill Book Company, 1968).

MOSSTON, MUSKA, *Developmental Movement* (Columbus, Ohio: Charles E. Merrill Books, Inc., 1965).

SMITH, HOPE M., ed., *Introduction to Human Movement* (Reading, Mass.: Addison-Wesley Publishing Co., 1968).

WELLS, KATHARINE F., *Kinesiology*, Third Edition (Philadelphia: W. B. Saunders Company, 1960).

chapter include (1) familiar happenings in the life of the child, (2) improvisation based upon an idea, which may be carried out in the child's own way, and (3) use of various sensory stimuli.

The term "movement exploration" is commonly defined as an approach to physical education, a method of teaching multiple movement patterns or skills. The technique most often used in movement exploration is that of questions or challenges introduced by phrases like "Who can ...?" "Can you ...?" "Find a way to ...," and "Let's all try to ..." Through questions and comments each child is encouraged to solve the problem in his own way. The teacher encourages imagination and individualism and avoids reprimand or negative evaluation.

Grade levels have not been assigned to these activities because they may be adapted to any developmental level. The clue to an exploratory or experimental response on the part of the child lies in the procedures used by the teacher in presenting the activities. Children vary in their abilities to move freely and independently. Some of them may need reassurance from the teacher; others may need help

MOVEMENT EXPLORATION

Exploratory movement involves the total organism in activities demanding varying amounts of space. To encourage exploratory behavior on the part of the child, it is important to engage his attention through new and interesting motivating stimuli. The desire to explore and invent is a natural force in childhood, for which the movement medium provides a natural vehicle for expression.

in understanding the problem by having the teacher rephrase it in a less complex way.

Familiar happenings in the life of the child may include stories, games, holidays, animals, toys, occupations, and the like. After a field trip, for example, children may be asked to show how things looked, how they moved, their relationships to each other in space. Movement might take the form of pantomime for younger children; for older children it might take the form of capturing the abstract qualities of speed, intensity, shape, or range of motion.

Improvisations may be exploratory, with children moving freely in response to varied stimuli. Music can serve as a source of free, improvisational movement that will help the child develop a feeling for form and an understanding of rhythmic elements. Children may also explore movement qualities such as swinging, percussive, sustained, vibratory, and collapsed movement. They may find pleasure in experimenting with movement, using qualities in juxtaposition, such as swinging and then collapsing.

Sensory stimulation (visual, auditory, tactile, gustatory, olfactory) may serve as a source of movement, either of a free, exploratory nature or in the composition of a dance.

Materials in other chapters of this book provide activities for exploring movement patterns related to coping with the environments of land, air, suspension, water, objects of location, time, and space. For example, a game of tag may present problems in moving on a particular surface in different directions, at varying rates of speed, and in relation to other moving children.

You?

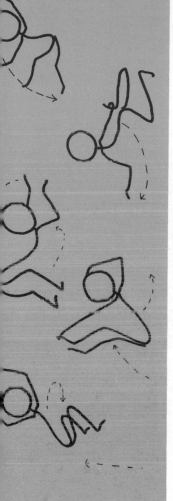

Players:
any number

Equipment:
none

Behavioral goal: To solve many different movement problems.

Children scatter around the area and each child sits in the middle of his own territory. They try to solve the movement problems or challenges given by the teacher or another child. The teacher may start by giving several movement problems; then each child may take a turn at giving a movement problem for the others to solve. Challenges may include:

1. Can you sit on the floor and move your head up and down?

2. Can you move your shoulders up and down?

3. Can you move your whole body up and down?

4. Can you walk in a small circle?

5. Can you move in a small circle using only one hand and one foot?

6. Can you sit on the floor and touch your head to your knees?

7. Can you turn around without leaving your sitting position?

Movement Exploration: any level   9

8. Can you make a high bridge with your body?
9. Can you curl into a very small ball?
10. Can you wiggle your toes as you move your feet from side to side?
11. Can you twist your body from side to side?
12. Can you jump forward, then backward?
13. Can you move some part of your body while jumping in the air?

14. Can you clap your hands at the height of the jump?
15. Can you walk around your territory as though you were walking in molasses?
16. Can you hop around your territory as though you were hopping on ice?
17. Can you run among your classmates and back to your territory without touching anyone?

EVALUATIVE CHECK LIST

1. Is each child able to accept the challenge and solve the movement problem?

2. Is each child becoming innovative in finding his own movement rather than imitating others constantly?
   a. Does he have confidence in his own ability?
   b. Does he feel acceptance from teacher and group?

3. Can each child demonstrate the basic movements of bending, stretching, twisting? Is he aware that all other movement patterns are combinations of these three basic movements?

NOTES

Animals

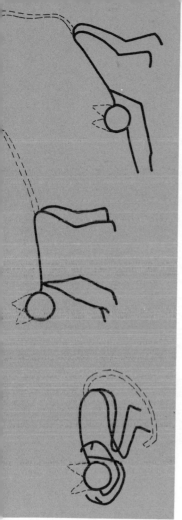

Players:
any number

Equipment:
none

Behavioral goal: To select a favorite animal and show how it moves.

Teacher and children list the names of animals or the chalk board. They might first visit the zoo and notice the different kinds of animals and how they move, or they might select farm or ranch animals, circus animals, or pets.

Teacher and children select one animal from the list and decide on its characteristic movements. For example, a cat has soft fur that stands up when the cat is frightened; it has a long tail, which it wraps around itself or carries high in the air; it is quick and leaps and jumps very high; it is very flexible and can curl into a small ball or stretch out very long.

Children explore movement that characterizes each animal as different traits are discussed. For example, after discussing the cat they may try leaping, curling into a ball, and stretching. Then each child chooses one animal and works out movement patterns that show how his animal moves.

EVALUATIVE CHECK LIST

1. Are children able to identify the distinctive qualities of different animals?

2. Are children able to translate into movement the distinctive qualities of different animals?

3. Is each child able to move in many different ways that characterize his animal? Does the movement distinguish his animal from the others?

NOTES

Characters

Players:
any number

Equipment:
none

Behavioral goal: To move in a way that describes the characters in the story.

Teacher and children select characters from a favorite story. They describe the characters in movement terms, such as slow, fast, light, twisted, smooth, floating, shaking.

Each child selects a favorite character and describes his character through movement. Children who have selected the same character may form a group and work out some movement sequences that describe the character.

Teacher reads the story aloud and children who have selected a certain character perform his action as it occurs in the story, using the movement that describes the character. It may be helpful to decide beforehand where certain action takes place; for example, if some of the action takes place in a house, the location of the "house" in the play area may be determined.

EVALUATIVE CHECK LIST

1. Does each child explore many ways to move that are typical of the character he has chosen?

2. Are several children able to work cooperatively in a group as they plan descriptive movement for a character?

3. Is each child able to move in his own way without fear of ridicule or criticism?

4. Are children able to move on the appropriate cue when the story is read?

NOTES

Playground

Players:
any number

Equipment:
none

Behavioral goal: To show playground activities and equipment in movement.

Children and teacher list playground activities on the chalkboard, such as kickball, softball, jungle gym, four square, bars, rings, and so on.

Each child selects a favorite activity and pantomimes how it is played. Then he pretends he is a piece of equipment used in the activity and shows in movement how the equipment looks and moves. For example, a child imitating a ball might roll on the floor, bounce up and down into the air, or stand up and spin while traveling forward.

Children accompany their movement with sounds. For example, a child who is pretending to jump rope might say, "Whish, whish," or he might chant a rhyme as he jumps.

EVALUATIVE CHECK LIST

1. Does each child explore freely as he tries to capture the quality of the equipment and activity through movement?

2. Is each child able to think of sounds or words to accompany himself and does he move rhythmically to his own accompaniment?

3. Do children enjoy showing their activities to the rest of the class?

NOTES

occupation

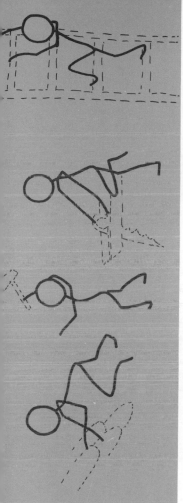

Players:
any number

Equipment:
none

Behavioral goal: To show through movement the kinds of things that people do in various occupations.

Teacher and children discuss the kinds of things people do in various occupations, such as fireman, policeman, teacher, housewife, truck driver, doctor, zoo keeper, singer, and the like. Children explore movement that shows how people do these things. For example, a "fireman" might pretend to slide down a pole, drive a fire truck, manipulate a hose, or climb a ladder.

Each child decides what he would like to be when he grows up and plans a sequence of movements that would

describe his occupation. When children have decided on their actions, the teacher helps them explore variations in movement by setting problems for them:

1. *How fast can you perform your movement sequence?*
2. *How slow can you perform your movement sequence?*
3. *How large can you make your movements?*
4. *How small can you make your movements?*

5. *In what directions can you move?*

6. *How high can you perform your movement sequence?*

7. *How low can you perform your movement sequence?*

8. *Can you use a different part of your body in performing your movement sequence?*

9. *Can you accompany yourself with sounds?*

EVALUATIVE CHECK LIST

1. Is each child able to find many ways of showing his occupation through movement?

2. Is each child able to select a sequence of movements to show his occupation?

3. Does each child respond to the teacher's questions with many variations in movement?

4. Is each child able to move rhythmically to his own accompaniment?

NOTES

Ideas

Players:
any number

Equipment:
none

Behavioral goal: To choose a holiday object and describe it through movement.

Teacher and children select a holiday and make a list of objects and a list of feelings that describe the holiday. For example, objects related to Halloween may include black cats arching their backs and hissing, witches riding on broomsticks or stirring cauldrons, owls hooting in trees, a smiling jack-o-lantern, bats flying through the sky, children dressed in costumes for trick-or-treat. Feelings may be merry, spooky, stealthy, scary, excited, happy.

Each child chooses a favorite object and shows what it looks like in movement and how it feels. Children might move to show the shape of the object or they might draw the object in space using different parts of the body (head, elbow, knee) as the pencil. They might move to show the movement quality of the object (bats sailing and darting through space, or black cats stealthily slinking through space, then collapsing to sleep).

Children who have related objects may form groups and make a dance to show to the others in the class, accompanying themselves with percussion instruments, records, songs, or voice sounds.

EVALUATIVE CHECK LIST

1. Is each child able to choose an object and express his feeling about it through movement?

2. Does each child experiment with many ways of moving in the shape or quality of his object?

3. Are children able to cooperate in group action to show how their objects look in movement?

4. Is each child able to accompany himself and others with sounds, songs, or other forms of accompaniment?

NOTES

Directions
and
Levels

Players:
any number

Equipment:
none

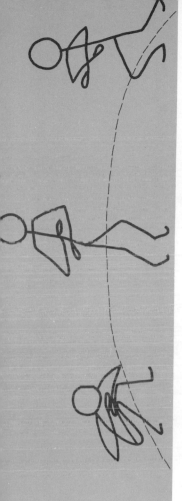

Behavioral goal: To experiment with moving in different directions and levels.

Children move in many different directions, such as forward, backward, sideward, diagonal, around. Children explore up and down and in-between. For example, "down" may be lying on the floor and "up" may be standing, with "in-between" either sitting or kneeling. Then, using a body part, such as an arm, they show up and down and in-between.

Children explore directions and levels, using locomotion. For example, they may walk forward in a circle with the body as low as possible, then move backward on a diagonal with the body in-between, then jump in a circle with the body as high as possible. They may repeat the pattern several times, fast and then slow, with small and large movements.

Children select a game using levels and directions and act it out in movement. For example, softball uses different directions and levels, with the batter reaching for a high or low ball, the baseman running backward to field a high fly or forward to field a grounder, the catcher reaching for a high, wild pitch, and so on.

EVALUATIVE CHECK LIST

1. Is each child able to move in many different directions and at many different levels?

2. Is each child able to create a pattern that can be repeated several times with changes in range and time, such as large, small and fast, slow?

3. Are children able to work together in pantomiming a game that uses varying directions and levels?

NOTES

People

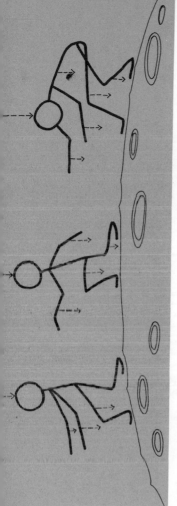

Players:
any number

Equipment:
none

Behavioral goal: To pretend one is a space person and experiment with slow and fast movement.

Children pretend they are on a planet in space where they are much heavier than on earth. They lift an arm as though it were very heavy and walk as though their bodies were twice as heavy as they are.

Children pretend they are on the moon, where their bodies are much lighter than on earth. They move body parts as though they were very light and walk as though their bodies were very light.

Children select a familiar game such as tag, softball, or dodgeball and play the game on the strange planet, using slow motion because of their increased weight. The teacher may use a gong to help the children maintain sustained movement; each movement should continue for as long as the child can hear the sound of the gong.

Children then act out the movements in speeded-up motion.

Movement Exploration: any level   23

EVALUATIVE CHECK LIST

1. Is each child able to move in many different ways using a sustained quality? Does he maintain a slow, consistent tempo?

2. Is each child able to move lightly and quickly in a faster tempo?

3. Is each child able to manage the smooth, controlled quality while moving in the game with others?

4. Is each child able to repeat his movement in a fast, quick tempo while in the game with others?

5. Are children able to contrast slow, sustained movements and light, quick movements, changing easily from one tempo to another?

NOTES

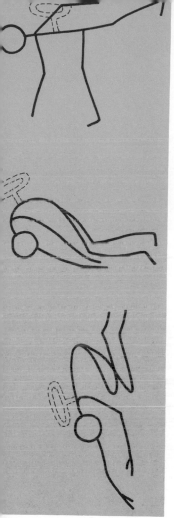

Behavioral goal: To move like a wind-up toy and collapse when the toy "runs down."

Children pretend they are wind-up toys, such as dolls, dogs, monkeys, rabbits, clowns. Teacher winds up the toys and the children begin moving at a brisk pace, getting slower and slower until they are completely "run down" and stop or collapse to the floor. Teacher or a child rewinds the toys and the sequence is repeated.

Children explore moving in the manner of many kinds of wind-up toys, using both locomotor and non-locomotor movement. For example, a child may be a toy monkey who hops up and down and claps his hands together, a toy bear who beats a toy drum, or a toy soldier who marches a few steps with his gun on his shoulder. Children might bring their wind-up toys to school to stimulate other ideas.

EVALUATIVE CHECK LIST

1. Are children able to change gradually from fast movement to slow, sustained movement as the toy "runs down?"

2. Are children able to topple over or collapse slowly and gradually? Are they able to collapse quickly?

3. Are children inventive in working out interesting movement to characterize the toy?

a. Do they explore both locomotor and non-locomotor movement?

b. Do they move in different directions and at different levels?

NOTES

Behavioral goal: To explore many ways of collapsing.

Teacher explains that collapsing a body part or the whole body means relaxing a body part or the whole body, allowing gravity to pull it down to the earth. Children stand and stretch tall, then collapse (relax) one part at a time slowly, first the fingertips, then the wrists, elbows, arms, head and shoulders, and so on until they are left collapsed on the floor.

Children lie on floor with eyes closed. Teacher slowly and quietly tells them that they are sawdust dolls with a hole in the toe, and the sawdust is slowly running out of each part of the body; first the hands, then the arms, head, shoulders, chest, hips, and so on until the children are completely collapsed on the floor. Children try a fast collapse, starting from a sitting position and falling to the floor, then from the knees to the floor, and finally from a standing position to the floor.

Children move around the room and on the teacher's signal they stop and collapse one body part. Children explore collapsing other isolated parts of the body by moving to music or a drum beat, collapsing just one part each time the music stops. They may select ideas for collapsing in different ways, such as gradually becoming tired; suddenly becoming exhausted; being rag dolls falling to the floor; being puppets dropped by the puppet master; being a balloon being pricked with a pin; being a tire blowing out or going down with a slow leak.

EVALUATIVE CHECK LIST

1. Does each child understand the effect of gravity on objects on the earth?

2. Does each child understand that relaxation is the release of tension in the muscles?

3. Is each child able to relax all parts of his body while lying on the floor?

   a. Are the eyes closed?

   b. Are feet and ankles relaxed?

   c. Are head and shoulders relaxed?

4. Is each child able to collapse an isolated part of the body?

5. Is each child able to collapse gradually? Rapidly? From different levels?

NOTES

Head
Is a
Swing

Players:
any number

Equipment:
none

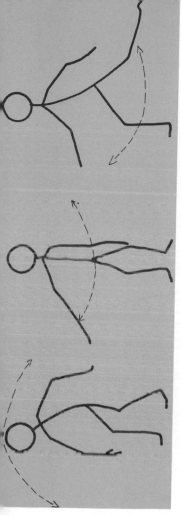

Behavioral goal: To swing the body in many different ways.

Children and teacher chant, "My head is a swing and it swings and swings and swings . . ." as they swing their heads up and down, side to side, around and around, allowing the head to fall as far as possible each time.

They continue to swing other body parts as they chant:

My arm is a swing . . . .
Both arms are swings . . . .
My trunk is a swing . . . .
My leg is a swing . . . .

They travel backward and forward and sideward as they continue to swing various body parts. As they swing the arms upward they allow the body to move upward in a leap or jump. The body is a part of every swing. Teacher and children list things that swing, such as an elephant's trunk, a train signal, a playground swing, and the pendulum of a clock. Children work with a partner or in groups as they show with their own swing patterns the idea of something that swings.

EVALUATIVE CHECK LIST

1. Do children swing with a relaxed movement?
   a. Do they use force to start the swing and allow momentum to carry it through?
   b. Do they "give in" to gravity on downward movements?

2. Are children able to swing different parts of the body?

3. Do children allow the entire body to be a part of the swing, even though one body part is providing impetus for the swing?

4. Are children able to travel as they swing?

5. Are children able to work out their own swing patterns?

NOTES

Am a Hammer

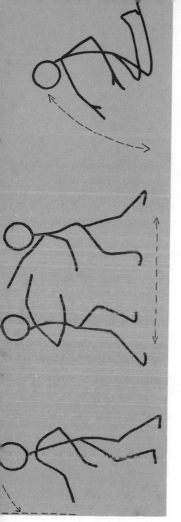

Players:
any number

Equipment:
none

Behavioral goal: To pretend one is a hammer and move with a percussive quality.

Children pretend their heads are hammers and pretend to hammer a nail into the wall. They continue exploring percussive movement by using other body parts as hammers.

Children select other ideas for exploring percussive movement, such as pretending to knock on a door, stamp a peg into the ground, jump on something to break it, pop bubble gum. Children work together to show sudden, sharp movement. For example, two children may act out a fist fight by facing each other, one advancing with percussive steps and striking at the other as the second child retreats with percussive steps, dodging with percussive movements of the body.

EVALUATIVE CHECK LIST

1. Are children able to use sudden, sharp (percussive) movements that stop abruptly?

2. Are children able to work cooperatively in exploring ideas to use movement with a percussive quality?

3. Are children able to contrast percussive movement and swinging movement? Percussive movement and collapsing?

NOTES

Am an Electric Toothbrush

Players:
any number

Equipment:
none

Behavioral goal: To pretend that one is an electric toothbrush and vibrate the whole body; to explore other ways of vibrating.

Teacher has children hold an electric toothbrush or some other kind of electric vibrator. Children try to vibrate isolated parts of the body by pretending that their fingers, hands, arms, heads, and so on are the electric toothbrush. Then they see how many of the body parts they can vibrate together.

Children explore other ideas using vibratory movement, such as holding a rivet machine, shaking water off

one's body parts like a dog, riding on a bumpy road, taking off in a rocket, shaking with cold. They may try travelling as they vibrate body parts, shaking isolated parts of the body, then combining the vibrating parts. They might also explore contrasting movement, such as riding on a smooth road and suddenly coming upon a bumpy section, or taking off in a rocket that shakes and vibrates and then moves smoothly out into space.

EVALUATIVE CHECK LIST

1. Is each child able to vibrate isolated parts of the body: for example, shaking water off the foot, the hand, the head?

2. Is each child able to vibrate the entire body, as in riding over a bumpy road?

3. Is each child able to vibrate as he travels through space?

4. Is each child able to contrast vibratory movement with other movement qualities, such as sustained, swinging, percussive?

NOTES

Qualities

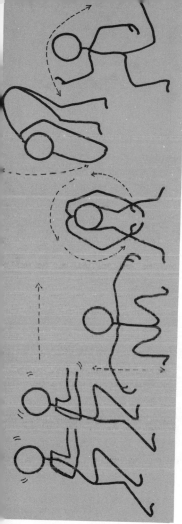

Players:
any number

Equipment:
none

Behavioral goal: To explore movement qualities using ideas.

Children use ideas to stimulate movement, illustrating different qualities. For example:

1. Using the trunk as the pendulum of a clock, swing rhythmically from side to side. The clock begins to run down until the pendulum is moving in slow motion. Suddenly, the spring snaps and parts of the clock shoot off percussively. The spring vibrates by itself.

2. An old freight train is chugging along, vibrating as it goes over the bumpy track. The signal begins to swing at the crossing, the train slows down, and the whistle in the signal tower pops up and down percussively.

3. A horse trots in short, quick percussive movements, swinging its head from side to side impatiently. It slows down and stops, gets to its knees, lies on its side, and rolls from side to side.

4. A sailboat sails smoothly on the ocean, the waves swinging it rhythmically from side to side. It crosses the wake

of another boat, bumping percussively up and down. A sudden breeze whips the sail about and the boat shudders and vibrates until it rights itself, then sails smoothly on.

5. The wheel of the sewing machine swings round and round, the needle bobs up and down in short, percussive jabs on the cloth, which moves slowly through the machine.

EVALUATIVE CHECK LIST

1. Are children able to think of dramatic ideas for showing the movement qualities (swinging, percussive, sustained, vibratory, collapsed)?

2. Are children able to show different qualities of movement and to change from quality to quality?

3. Do children experiment with both locomotor and non-locomotor movement as they explore movement qualities?

4. Do children use varied directions and levels?

NOTES

Shapes

Players:
any number

Equipment:
none

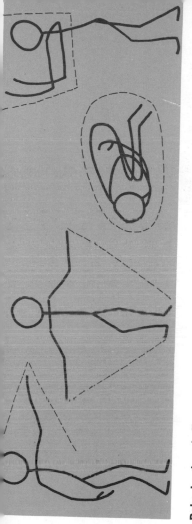

Behavioral goal: To experiment with different ways of making shapes in space.

Children explore different body shapes as the teacher gives them problems similar to these:

1. *Can you make your body into a point, using the whole body?*

2. *Can you make your arms into a point, your leg, your elbow and knees?*

3. *Can you make your whole body into a ball?*

4. *Can you make your arms into a ball? Your legs? Your head and shoulders?*

5. *Can you make your whole body into a brick wall?*

6. *Can you make your arm into a brick wall? Your leg? Your shoulder?*

Children explore different air shapes that can be made by movement as the teacher gives them problems similar to these:

7. *Can you make a curved shape in the air, using your whole body?*

Children draw pictures of objects in space, using the whole body as the pencil, then using isolated body parts, such as elbow, nose, knee. Children experiment with space pictures, starting the picture with one part of the body as the pencil, and completing it with other parts of the body.

Children make shapes in space, varying range and speed, such as making shapes using very small, then very large movements, and using very quick, then very slow movements.

8. *Can you make a curved shape in the air, using various parts of your body?*

9. *Can you make a straight line in the air?*

10. *Can you make a square in the air?*

11. *Can you make a round shape in the air?*

12. *Can you make a triangular shape in the air?*

13. *Can you make a twisted shape in the air?*

14. *Can you make a spiral in the air?*

15. *What new shapes can you make by combining curves, squares, lines, and so on?*

EVALUATIVE CHECK LIST

1. Is each child able to accept the challenges given by the teacher and explore many space shapes?

2. Is each child innovative in using many different parts of his body in making space pictures?

3. Does each child vary movement qualities, such as using sustained movement for long, smooth lines and percussive movement for sharp, jagged lines, and so on?

4. Does each child vary range and speed of movement, using large and small, and quick and slow movements?

5. Does each child vary movement patterns such as running, throwing, crawling, and so on as he makes his space shapes?

6. Is each child experimenting with moving in ways that are new to him?

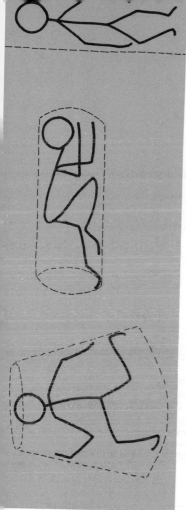

the Jelly Glass

Players:
any number

Equipment:
none

Behavioral goal: To lie on the bottom of a "jelly glass" and explore the sides for cracks; to explore different shapes and sizes.

Children imagine they are lying on the bottom of a jelly glass. The glass is just large enough for them to touch its sides in every direction by stretching as hard as possible?

Children explore the sides of the jelly glass for cracks. Lying on the bottom they explore all sides carefully by stretching as far as possible. Then very slowly, moving up from the bottom, they explore all sides carefully by stretching as far as possible. After their exploration, they break out of the jelly glass by kicking the sides and breaking the glass.

Children experiment with different shapes in space by pretending to explore:

1. the sides of a box;

2. a very low tunnel which they go through by creeping, crawling, or moving on the stomach;

3. the sides of a high, narrow tunnel which they can get

through only by standing and moving sideways, making themselves as thin as possible;

EVALUATIVE CHECK LIST

1. Do children stretch all body parts as far as possible as they explore various shapes?

2. Do children explore stretching at various levels (lying, sitting, kneeling, standing)?

3. Do children find interesting ways of exploring for

4. other objects, such as a mailbox, letter-holder, ice cream cone, apothecary jar, top drawer of a desk, and so on.

cracks, such as with the feet, hands, nose, elbow, knee, and so on?

4. Do children experiment with many different shapes, such as round, oval, square, triangle, tunnel, and so on?

NOTES

Name
Is . . .

Players:
any number

Equipment:
large sheets of paper; pencils or crayon

Behavioral goal: To form letters in space; to experiment with moving in various floor patterns, alone and with others.

Each child writes his own name on an imaginary chalkboard with an imaginary piece of chalk. Then he writes his name with the chalk attached to his elbow, then to his head, knee, foot.

Child writes his name on the floor by walking it as a floor pattern. He writes it as if he felt sad, happy, angry, tired, and so on.

Each child draws a simple, unbroken line on a piece of paper. Then he walks in a floor pattern corresponding to his line.

Two children work together, drawing two lines that overlap or cross each other. Each child moves in a floor pattern corresponding to one of the lines. Then three children work together, each with his own line crossing or paralleling the others, and all moving on their individual floor patterns corresponding to their lines.

EVALUATIVE CHECK LIST

1. Is each child able to make interesting combinations of movements in writing his name?

2. Is each child able to translate his line drawings into floor patterns?

3. Are children able to work together in combining their line drawings into floor patterns?

4. Are children innovative in moving on their floor patterns in different ways?

   a. Do they move in different directions, such as forward, backward, sideward?

   b. Do they move in different levels, such as high, low?

   c. Do they use different qualities, such as vibratory, swinging, percussive?

NOTES

Objects

Players:
any number

Equipment:
none

Children and teacher list inanimate objects on the chalk-board. Children show with their bodies the shapes of the various objects. If the object is moved by an external force, they show with their bodies how the object would move.

Behavioral goal: To show with one's body the shapes of objects and how they move.

For instance, they may imitate the movement of:

1. *an orange being peeled;*
2. *a standing lamp being carried across the room;*
3. *a wall with a vine growing over it;*
4. *a paper clip being inserted on paper;*
5. *an ice cube melting;*
6. *a balloon with air coming out of it;*
7. *a cloud drifting through the sky, slowly changing shapes;*
8. *smoke coming out of a chimney;*
9. *a twisted pin being thrust into paper;*
10. *a rubber ball bouncing along the ground;*
11. *a boat being tossed by the waves;*
12. *an arrow being shot through the air;*
13. *a steel bar being hammered into different shapes.*

EVALUATIVE CHECK LIST

1. Are children able to identify the external forces that may move inanimate objects, such as wind, pull of gravity, water currents, animate objects?

2. Do children explore many different shapes with their bodies?

3. Do children experiment with many different ways of moving?

a. Do they bend in the direction the external force is moving them?

b. Do they move fast or slow, depending upon the amount of force being exerted?

NOTES

or

Smooth

Players:
any number

Equipment:
objects of varying textures

Behavioral goal: To touch various objects and show through movement how they make one feel.

Teacher discusses tactile sensitivity with children. Objects of varying textures are available, such as silk cloth, burlap, feathers, rope, seashells, mirrors, balls, driftwood, beads, furry slippers, and so on.

Children form small groups and each group receives an object. Each child shows how the object makes him feel. For example, a feather may make him feel soft, smooth, and light. He may stand in a straight line with his arms and legs extended, then move softly with his arms waving gently from side to side.

EVALUATIVE CHECK LIST

1. Are children able to identify differences in texture?

2. Are children inventive in showing the way the textures feel to them?

3. Are children able to work cooperatively in organizing movement patterns to describe the textures?

    a. Do they move in different directions and levels?

    b. Do they move at different tempos?

    c. Do they use movement quality to characterize their textures?

NOTES

Am
a
Color

Players:
any number

Equipment:
different-colored objects

Behavioral goal: To show in movement: how a color makes one feel.

Objects of many different colors are available, such as a colored scarf, hat, box, construction paper, tissue paper, and the like. Teacher holds up a colored object and all discuss how the color makes them feel. If the shape of the object appears to influence the feeling, the teacher may use only colored paper.

Teacher might ask questions like these:

1. What do you think of when you see blue?

2. Does blue make you feel like moving fast or slow?

3. Does blue make you feel open or closed?

4. Does blue make you feel happy? shivery? angry? sunny? hot? cold?

5. Does blue make you feel small or large?

Children move in the ways that the colors make them feel, alone and with others.

EVALUATIVE CHECK LIST

1. Is each child innovative in choosing movement that shows his feeling about a color?

2. Does he explore many movement possibilities, using different directions, levels, large and small spaces, different movement qualities?

3. Is each child able to move without copying others?

NOTES

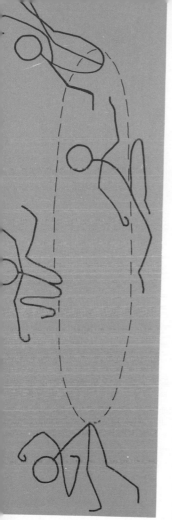

and
Smell

Players:
any number

Equipment:
none

Behavioral goal: To move in ways that tastes and smells make one feel.

Teacher and children discuss various tastes and smells, describing them and telling how they would feel in movement. Some responses may be:

1. *The taste of lemon makes me feel all scrunched together and shivery.*
2. *Mother's perfume makes me feel good, like dancing.*
3. *Chocolate candy tastes like jumping up and down.*
4. *A carnation smell feels like turning around and waving my arms.*
5. *A cake baking in the oven smells like hugging myself and swaying.*

Children choose a favorite taste or smell. They show how it makes them feel in non-locomotion, like sitting and swaying up and down, and in locomotion, like traveling across the room. For example, a child may decide that a lemon makes him feel small, wrinkled and shivery. He may sit on the floor, hunching his shoulders, bringing his head to his knees, clenching his fists, and moving from side to side. He may repeat the movement, rising to his knees, to his feet, and traveling through space with some form of locomotion.

EVALUATIVE CHECK LIST

1. Does each child explore many movement possibilities in describing how things smell and taste?
   a. Does he move in different directions and levels?
   b. Does he use large and small spaces?
   c. Does he use many different movement qualities?

2. Is each child learning to use his body as an instrument of communication through movement?

3. Is each child demonstrating independence and freedom of choice in developing his own movement patterns?

NOTES

Players:
any number

Equipment:
percussion

Behavioral goal: To echo a rhythm pattern by moving in different ways.

Teacher beats a rhythm pattern, using a percussion instrument or clapping with her hands. Children echo the rhythm pattern by moving their bodies. Teacher may suggest a movement, such as walk, hop, swing, push and pull, or children may choose their own movements.

Child may be leader and perform or beat a rhythm pattern for others to echo.

Examples of rhythm patterns:

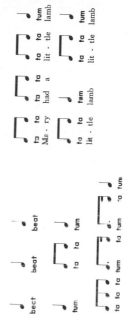

Movement Exploration: any level   51

EVALUATIVE CHECK LIST

1. Are children able to echo patterns accurately?

2. Are children able to echo increasingly longer and more complex patterns?

3. Are children able to beat or clap the rhythm patterns of songs or poems?

4. Is each child able to take the leader's part and beat a pattern for others to echo?

5. Are children innovative in finding movements to fit the pattern?

6. Do children vary levels, directions, and qualities of movement?

NOTES

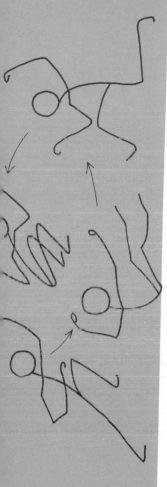

Players:
any number

Equipment:
none

Behavioral goal: To move to a song, alone and with others.

Teacher and children select a familiar round and sing it several times together and in round form, if they are able. Examples of rounds are "Little Tommy Tinker," "White Coral Bells," "Three Blind Mice," "Row, Row, Row Your Boat," "Ten Little Indians."

Children plan a movement pattern for each line of the round, then move together as they sing the song until they are familiar with the movement patterns.

Children may use round form, with one group singing and moving to the first phrase followed by other groups in succession until the song is completed.

EVALUATIVE CHECK LIST

1. Is each child able to plan interesting movements for each line of the round?

2. Is each child able to perform his movement patterns for the round and accompany himself by singing?

3. Do children work together cooperatively in learning and performing the round?

4. Do children experiment with varied levels, directions, and qualities of movement?

NOTES

RUNNING AND CHASING

Running activities contribute to the development and maintenance of organic endurance, depending upon how they are performed. If the purpose is to develop endurance, the activities should include running for increasingly longer periods of time or at faster speeds.

Tagging activities emphasize the skills of starting and stopping, dodging, changing direction, running with the body at varying levels, and maintaining and

rapidly. The individual being chased must be able to swerve, start rapidly, stop and change direction, stretch away from the chaser, bend and duck under the hand of the chaser, and so on. The chaser must be able to anticipate the action of the one he is trying to tag, to move with him, to block his movement, and to overtake and tag him successfully.

Running occurs when the center of gravity of the body is displaced forward to the degree that the period of double support by the feet becomes a period of non-support. This displacement can be observed as increased body lean, and is proportional to the speed of running. Excessive bouncing or raising the center of gravity reduces the speed of running. Bending the knees to shorten the length of the limbs, on the other hand, increases speed. The elbows should be flexed in order to permit faster arm swings for eliminating undesirable sideward movements.

When running, an individual who wishes to stop or change direction must slow down until he can achieve sufficient contact with the ground to change direction. Moving the center of gravity to a position perpendicular or to the rear of the base of support permits a strong placement of the foot, with an increased friction surface. This, in turn, permits the use of the strong knee extensors in a lengthening contraction for deceleration. If the center of gravity is moved too far to the rear, the angle of foot placement permits slipping, and a sliding fall occurs. Falls are most likely to occur on blacktop in the vicinity of sand or small gravel.

Many four and five year olds may find tagging games difficult in both organization and skills. Movement exploration without high organization is more to their liking, particularly if there is adequate space for running, jumping, and moving with the whole body. When children progress in their skills and in their ability to understand game boundaries, rules, and formations, they are ready to perform successfully in tag games.

Older children enjoy games with more complex organization, which use many types of skills. They are more interested in adult sports, particularly at the fifth and sixth grade levels, and thoroughly enjoy participating in competitive team activities.

The games in this chapter are presented in order from simple to more difficult, and most children will enjoy the activities suggested for their own age levels.

Horses

Players:
10–20

Equipment:
none

Valley

Range

Behavioral goal: To run very fast from the "range" to the "valley."

Children are wild horses, grazing on the range. Suddenly, a mountain lion screams, frightening them. They run swiftly to the valley where they are safe. The lion may or may not give chase.

To develop endurance, this game may be repeated several times. Children try to run faster each time. Running distances may be gradually increased each successive day.

EVALUATIVE CHECK LIST

1. Does each child start immediately on signal and run directly to the "valley" as fast as he can?

2. Does each child understand how to start and stop quickly?
   a. Does he lean forward to start quickly?
   b. Does he bend knees and spread feet apart to stop quickly?

3. Does each child understand how to improve his running?

   a. Does he push off from the back foot?
   b. Does he land on the balls of the feet, knees easy?
   c. Does he swing his arms while running?

4. Does each child understand how to improve his endurance through running?
   a. Does he run a greater distance each time?
   b. Does he run faster each time?

NOTES

Players:
any number

Equipment:
none

Behavioral goal: To imitate a space ship and "orbit the earth" by running rapidly in a circle.

Children and teacher decide upon an object that will represent the earth, such as a tree, beanbag, circle, base, and so on. Children are space ships, and on the count-down, "Five, four, three, two, ONE!" the rockets blast the space ships off the ground; they quickly pick up speed and go into orbit around the earth.

After one or more orbits, space ships return and "splash down."

Game may be repeated any number of times, with space ships flying any number of orbits. To improve endurance, children try to run longer and faster each time.

EVALUATIVE CHECK LIST

1. Does each child understand how to start quickly?
   a. Does he lean forward?
   b. Does he push off from the back foot?

2. Is each child able to run rapidly in a circle?
   a. Can he carry the body forward?
   b. Can he lean toward the center of the circle?

3. Is each child able to run in his own orbit and avoid collision with other "space ships"?

4. Does each child understand how to improve his endurance through running?
   a. Does he run faster each time?
   b. Does he run a greater distance each time?

NOTES

Stop

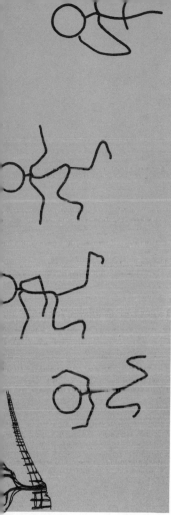

Players:
any number

Equipment:
whistle

Behavioral goal: To run on a signal and stop when the whistle blows; to solve the movement problems given by the teacher.

Children are scattered around the playing area. On the signal, "Run!" the children run in any direction until the whistle blows, then they stop immediately. They start again on the signal, "Run!"

Children must be able to run and stop on appropriate signals, staying within the boundaries and avoiding other runners. This game may be varied to explore directions, time, and many movement possibilities. For example:

1. Can you run in a circle and stop when the whistle blows?
2. Can you hop to your right and stop when the whistle blows?
3. Can you walk like an elephant and stop when the whistle blows?
4. Can you run sideward toward the school?
5. Can you skip toward the teacher?
6. When whistle blows, can you stop and clap your hands?
7. When the whistle blows, can you stop and do a trick?

EVALUATIVE CHECK LIST

1. Does each child understand how to start and stop quickly?
   a. Does he lean forward to start quickly?
   b. Does he bend knees and spread feet to stop quickly?

2. Does each child understand how to improve his endurance through running?
   a. Is he learning to run faster?
   b. Is he learning to run for a longer period of time?

3. Is each child able to follow directions, starting and stopping on signal?

4. Are children able to avoid running into others?
   a. Do they watch for others?
   b. Do they change direction quickly when necessary?
   c. Do they carry body weight forward to avoid falling?

NOTES

Run

Players:
10–20

Equipment:
none

Behavioral goal : To do as many "tiger runs" as possible, trying to increase the number each day.

Two goals are marked, 20–30 feet apart. Children stand back of one goal. Teacher says, "Tigers run once!" Children run to opposite goal. Teacher says, "Tigers run twice!" Children run back to original goal. Teacher continues to call, "Tigers run three times!" and so on until children tire.

A record may be kept of the number of "tiger runs" and each succeeding day the children try for more runs.

As they improve in endurance, the distance between the goals may be lengthened.

EVALUATIVE CHECK LIST

1. Does each child understand how to improve his endurance?

   a. Does he run as fast as possible?

   b. Does he run farther each day?

   c. Is he improving his running skill?

2. Is each child able to follow directions, starting and running on signal to the specified goal?

NOTES

Tag

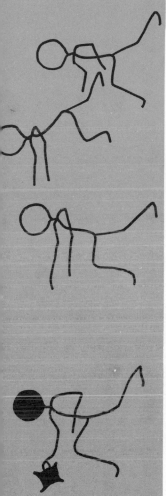

Players:
8–10 per group

Equipment:
1 beanbag per group

Behavioral goal: To overtake and tag the player with the beanbag; to avoid being tagged if one is IT.

Children all chase IT, who is carrying a beanbag. If someone tags IT, the tagger takes the beanbag and becomes IT, and other children chase him.

If IT chooses to do so, he may toss the beanbag away at any time. The child who catches or picks up the beanbag is IT and is chased by the others.

EVALUATIVE CHECK LIST

1. Do children know how to dodge effectively by changing direction quickly?

   a. Can they shift weight to the foot which is away from the direction of movement, freeing the opposite foot to step in the new direction?

   b. Can they lower the center of gravity by bending the knees, providing a stronger push-off toward the new direction?

2. Do children have the endurance they need to continue running until tagged?

3. Do children show determination in their attempts to catch IT?

   a. Do they run purposefully?

   b. Do they continue chasing until IT is caught?

4. Does the skillful player share with others by throwing or dropping the beanbag after he has shown that he could keep it?

NOTES

In the Sea

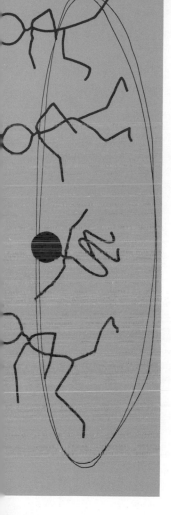

Players:
8–10 per group

Equipment:
none

Behavioral goal: To see how close one can get to the Frog without being tagged.

One child is the Frog and sits in the center of a circle. Other children dare the frog by running in close to him and saying, "Frog in the sea, can't catch me!"

If a child is tagged by the Frog, he also becomes a Frog and sits in the circle beside the first Frog. Frogs must tag from a sitting position. The game continues until four players are tagged. Then the first Frog chooses a new Frog from the players who were not tagged.

EVALUATIVE CHECK LIST

1. Do children understand how to move quickly to avoid being tagged?

a. Do they center body weight on foot which is away from the direction of movement?

b. Do they push off strongly, keeping weight low?

c. Do they keep feet in stride position to help maintain balance?

2. Does each child accept the challenge to "dare" by entering the circle frequently?

3. Do Frogs tag without being rough? Do they work together to tag others?

4. Does each child know what to do when he is tagged?

NOTES

Walk, Run

Players:
8–10 per group

Equipment:
none

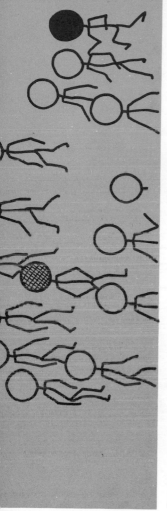

Behavioral goal: To move quickly to tag another and to avoid being tagged.

Children stand in a circle, facing the center. One child is IT and walks around outside the circle, chanting, "Walk, walk, walk," touching each player gently on the shoulder as he passes them. When he touches a player and says "Run!" the player so touched chases him around the circle. If the chaser touches him before he can reach the chaser's place in the circle, he must go into the "mush pot," which is in the center of the circle, and must stay there until another child enters the mush pot.

If he is not tagged before reaching the chaser's place in the circle, he stays in the new circle position. In either instance the chaser becomes the new IT, and the game continues.

Variations: this may be used for exploring other types of locomotor skills; for example, IT may say, "Walk, walk, walk, Skip!" or "Hop, Gallop, Slide," and so on.

EVALUATIVE CHECK LIST

1. Is each child in the circle ready to move quickly in the correct direction if IT chooses him?

2. Do circle players assume responsibility for maintaining the vacant spot in the circle?

3. Is each child able to run rapidly in a circle?
   a. Does he carry the body forward?
   b. Does he lean toward the center of the circle?

   c. Does he avoid touching or holding other circle players as he runs?

4. Does each child have the endurance to run swiftly around the circle without tiring?

5. Are children able to accept defeat if they are tagged and go to the center of the circle without argument or alibi?

NOTES

Runners

Players:
6–8 per group

Equipment:
none

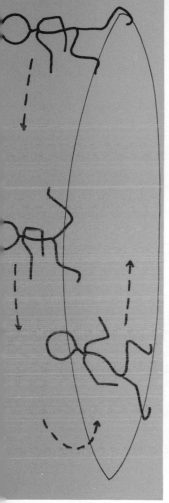

Behavioral goal: To improve endurance by running farther each day.

A large oval area, the "track," is marked off on the playground. A starting line is marked on the track. The children run around the track as many times as they can without stopping. When they are tired, they stop and tell the teacher how many full circles they completed.

The teacher may keep a chart that shows how many full circles each child completed. Each succeeding day, the children try to run farther than before. Each child should understand that the goal is to improve his own score, not to outdo everyone else in the class. Recognition should be given to each child who is able to improve his score, not to a class "winner."

EVALUATIVE CHECK LIST

1. Does each child understand how running a greater distance each time can improve his endurance? Does he understand how it:

   a. Strengthens the heart muscle by causing it to work harder?

   b. Improves circulation as more blood is pumped to the tissues?

   c. Improves lungs by causing them to breathe deeper to get needed oxygen?

   d. Helps him run longer without getting tired?

2. Does each child understand how to improve his running?

   a. Does he push off from the back foot?

   b. Does he land on the balls of the feet, knees easy?

   c. Does he swing arms easily?

3. Does each child work on improving his own score rather than competing with others in the class?

NOTES

Races

Players:
10–15 per group

Equipment:
none

Behavioral goal: To race faster than the other Jets.

Children are Jet Pilots and stand with both feet back of
starting line. On signal, "Take off!" Jets zoom to the
finish line. First Jet to cross the line is the winner, and
gives the signal for the next race.

EVALUATIVE CHECK LIST

1. Does each child know how to start and stop quickly?
   a. Does he lean forward to start quickly?
   b. Does he bend knees and spread feet to stop quickly?

2. Does each child know how to improve his running?
   a. Does he push off from the back foot?

   b. Does he land on the balls of the feet, knees easy?
   c. Does he swing arms easily with opposite foot forward?

3. Do children run across finish line at top speed, and stop *after* they are across?

NOTES

Goal

Players:
10–15 per group

Equipment:
none

Behavioral goal: To run fast on a signal and keep from being tagged.

One child is Huntsman and says to the other children, "Come with me to hunt tigers." The other children fall into line behind him and follow in his footsteps as he leads them away from the goal line.

When Huntsman says, "Bang!" the other children run to the goal as Huntsman tries to tag as many of them as possible. As each child is tagged, Huntsman calls out the child's name.

The Huntsman chooses a new Huntsman from the players who reached the base safely.

EVALUATIVE CHECK LIST

1. Does Huntsman think through the strategy of the situation before calling "Bang!"

   a. Does he lead the group as far from the goal as possible?

   b. Does he maneuver so he is between the goal and the group?

2. Do the children accept the "dare" of the game?

   a. Do they follow Huntsman closely?

   b. Do they take positions near the head of the line, close to the Huntsman?

   c. Do they follow closely in the footsteps of the person ahead of them?

3. Do children take off quickly on signal and run directly to the goal?

4. Is each child able to run swiftly without falling down or colliding with others?

5. Does each child have the endurance needed to continue running swiftly toward the goal, while dodging and avoiding the chaser?

NOTES

76

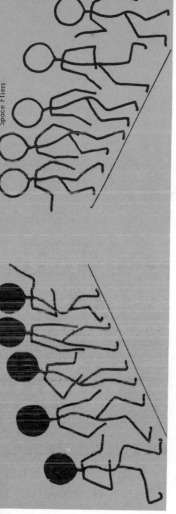

Space Fliers

in
Space

Players:
10–20 per group

Equipment:
none

Behavioral goal: To overtake and tag others; to avoid being tagged.

Half of the children are Earth Men and the other half are Space Fliers. Earth Men stand on one goal line and Space Fliers on the other. Space Fliers choose the name of an object that flies in space, like a rocket, spaceship, moon, planets, earth, meteor, astronaut, lunar module, and so on.

Space Fliers walk to a line 3 feet from the Earth Men and say, "Earth Men, who are we?" Earth Men guess until they guess the correct object, then they chase the

Space Fliers back to their goal. Any Fliers caught by the Earth Men become Earth Men and return to the goal with them. Space Fliers who were not caught choose a new space object and game continues until all are caught.

Game is repeated with original Earth Men becoming Space Fliers and original Fliers becoming Men.

EVALUATIVE CHECK LIST

1. Do children stay on their correct lines until the Space Fliers are guessed?

2. Are children able to take off quickly when the correct name is guessed?
   a. Do they push off hard from the back foot?
   b. Do they lean in the direction of movement?

3. Are children able to run swiftly without falling or colliding with others?

   a. Do they watch where they are going?
   b. Are they aware of positions of others?

4. Are children able to accept failure when tagged before reaching the goal, and become good-natured Earth Men?

5. Do children tag fairly without roughness or injury to others?

NOTES

Players:
12–20 per group

Equipment:
none

Behavioral goal: To overtake and tag others; to avoid being tagged.

Children stand behind one goal line. Child who is Dogcatcher stands in area between goals. Each child chooses the name of a dog, such as poodle, afghan, beagle, collie, and so on. The Dogcatcher calls, "Poodles run!" Children who are Poodles run to opposite goal as Dogcatcher tries to tag them. Any Poodle caught by Dogcatcher is put in the "dog pound."

After Dogcatcher has called several different names, he calls, "Dogs run!" All remaining children run to opposite goal. New Dogcatcher is chosen from among children who reached the goal safely, and game is repeated.

EVALUATIVE CHECK LIST

1. Is each child able to move quickly when his name is called?

2. Is each child able to dodge and change direction quickly to avoid being tagged?

a. Does he shift weight to the foot away from the direction of movement, freeing the opposite foot to step in the new direction?

b. Does he lower the center of gravity by bending the knees, providing a stronger push-off toward the new direction?

3. Does each child have the endurance to play the game successfully?

4. Is each child able to accept being tagged and assume responsibility for going to the "dog pound"?

5. Are children kind to those who are tagged, rather than teasing or critical toward them?

NOTES

Pullaway

Players:
12–20 per group

Equipment:
none

Behavioral goal: To overtake and tag runners; to avoid being tagged.

One child is IT and stands in the area between two goals. All other children are behind one goal line. IT calls, "Pom-pom-pullaway! Come away or I'll pull you away!" and all players must run to opposite goal. Any children who are caught help IT catch others, when he calls again. IT is the only player who can call.

When all children are caught, last one to be caught is the new IT. If it is difficult to judge which child is last one caught, IT may choose a new IT.

EVALUATIVE CHECK LIST

1. Do children respond to signal, moving only when IT calls?

2. Is each child able to dodge and change direction quickly to avoid being tagged, or to avoid collision with others?

   a. Does he lower the center of gravity by bending the knees?

   b. Does he push off from the back foot toward the new direction?

   c. Is he aware of positions of others, and does he watch where he is going?

3. Do children tag fairly without roughness or injury to others?

   a. Do they touch lightly?

   b. Are they ready to stop or change direction?

   c. Do they grip ground with feet to keep balance?

NOTES

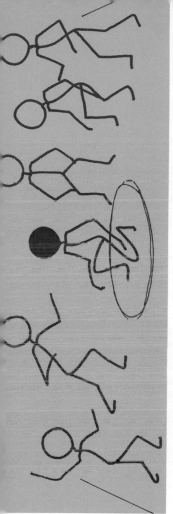

Players:
10–12 per group

Equipment:
none

Behavioral goal: To move quickly from sitting to running and overtake and tag others; to avoid being tagged.

One child is the Stone and sits in the center of a circle. Other children skip around the Stone. When Stone jumps up, players run to either goal and Stone chases them.

Any player tagged by Stone before reaching a goal becomes a Stone too, and sits in the circle with the first Stone. The other children continue to skip around the Stones. No Stone may move until the first Stone moves.

The game continues until all children are caught.

EVALUATIVE CHECK LIST

1. Is each child able to move quickly from sitting to standing to running?

2. Is each child able to move quickly from skipping to running when Stone jumps up and chases?

3. Does each child have the endurance to keep moving without undue fatigue?

4. Is each child developing the courage to "dare" and accept a challenge?

   a. Does he recognize his own limitations and skip close enough to Stone to be challenging but not fool-hardy?

   b. Does he appreciate the fact that the fun of the game is success with an element of danger?

NOTES

Many Orbits?

Players:
8–10 per group

Equipment:
name tags, box

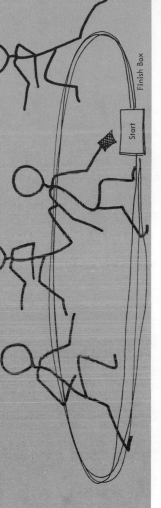

Behavioral goal: To run as many "orbits" as possible without stopping; to increase endurance by running a greater distance each day.

Children are Space Ships trying for an endurance record in circling the earth. Each Ship carries tags with the name of the Pilot (child who is the runner), and each time the ship completes an orbit, he drops a tag in a box at the starting point (or the teacher may check off the child's name on a chart as he runs past).

A record is kept from day to day so each child can see his increase in endurance as he is able to run greater distances. Comparisons are made with the child's own record, not against other runners.

EVALUATIVE CHECK LIST

1. Does each child understand how running a greater distance each time can improve his endurance? Does he understand how it:

   a. Strengthens the heart muscle by causing it to work harder?

   b. Improves circulation as more blood is pumped to the tissues?

   c. Improves lungs by causing them to breathe deeper to get needed oxygen?

   d. Help him run longer without getting tired?

2. Does each child understand how to improve his running?

   a. Does he push off from back foot?

   b. Does he land on balls of feet, knees easy?

   c. Does he swing arms easily?

   d. Does he bend knees and lean forward?

3. Does each child work on improving his own score rather than competing with others in the class?

NOTES

Dutchman

Players:
12–15 per group

Equipment:
none

Behavioral goal: To run swiftly with a partner.

Children stand in a circle, hands joined. Two children with hands joined are IT and walk around outside the circle. The child nearest the circle tags the joined hands of two circle players.

The IT couple runs around the circle in the same direction they were walking and the tagged couple, hands joined, runs around the circle in the direction opposite from the IT couple.

The couple first reaching the vacant place in the circle is IT for the next game.

EVALUATIVE CHECK LIST

1. Is each child ready to move quickly with a partner in the correct direction?

   a. Does he think of direction he is to move?

   b. Is he alert and aware of the position of the IT couple?

   c. Does he stand in readiness position, weight over both feet, knees easy, and in sideward stride position?

2. Do partners cooperate with each other while running?

   a. Do they help each other run faster?

   b. Do they keep each other from falling?

   c. Do they encourage each other?

   d. Does each accept defeat without blaming the other?

   e. Do they accept each other's limitations graciously?

3. Are couples able to meet and pass each other without breaking speed or colliding?

4. Is each child able to run rapidly in a circle?

   a. Does he carry body weight forward?

   b. Does he lean toward the center of the circle?

5. Do circle players assume responsibility for maintaining the vacant spot in the circle?

NOTES

from
Mars

Players:
10–12 per group

Equipment:
none

Behavioral goal: To overtake and tag another; to avoid being tagged.

One child is Man from Mars and stands in the center of the playing area. The other children stand on a boundary line and call, "Man from Mars, may we chase you to the stars?"

Man from Mars responds, "Yes, if you're wearing blue." All children wearing blue chase Man from Mars around the play area, all players staying within the predetermined boundaries. The child who tags him is the new Man from Mars and the game starts again.

Man from Mars may respond with any color or he may respond with colored objects, such as red shoes, black socks, yellow jewelry, white sweater, and so on.

EVALUATIVE CHECK LIST

1. Does each child have the endurance to keep running until the Man from Mars is tagged?

2. Are children able to avoid collisions while chasing IT?

3. Does each child think through and anticipate where IT is going to run, and move purposefully to intercept him?

4. Do successive ITs call different colors so that all children get to run?

NOTES

in
the
Pit

Players:
10–12 per group

Equipment:
none

Behavioral goal: To break out of the circle and avoid being tagged; to overtake and tag a runner.

One child is the Bear and stands inside the circle or "pit." He tries to break out of the circle by crawling under, stepping over, or breaking through the arms and hands of the circle players. When the Bear breaks out, the other players chase him around the play area. The child who catches him is the new Bear.

EVALUATIVE CHECK LIST

1. Does each child have the endurance needed to keep chasing until the Bear is caught?

2. Does each child have the strength and agility to break out of the "pit" when he is the Bear?

   a. Is he able to change position quickly, pretending to crawl under and then go over the hands?

   b. Is he able to change direction quickly, moving rapidly from one part of the circle to another?

   c. Is he able to force circle players to "break" hands?

3. Do children cooperate in reorganizing the circle efficiently when the Bear is caught?

   a. Do they come together quickly?

   b. Do they stand willingly in any place in the circle?

   c. Do they join hands with anyone?

NOTES

the Sheep

Players:
12–15 per group

Equipment:
none

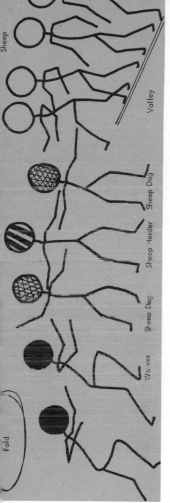

Behavioral goal: To guard the Sheep from the Wolves; to overtake and tag another; to avoid being tagged.

Two children are Wolves, one child is Sheep Dog, one child is Sheepherder. All other children are Sheep. The Sheep are grazing in the valley until the Sheepherder calls out, "Wolves!" The Sheep try to get to the fold without being caught by the Wolves. Sheepherder and Sheep Dog try to protect the Sheep from the Wolves by placing themselves between Sheep and Wolves. The Wolves try to dodge around them and tag as many Sheep as possible.

Wolves, Sheepherder, and Sheep Dog may not touch, push, or rough each other. New Wolves, Sheepherder, and Sheep Dog are chosen from among Sheep which were not caught.

EVALUATIVE CHECK LIST

1. Do Sheepherder and Sheep Dog use guarding skills in protecting the Sheep?
   a. Do they stay between Sheep and Wolves?
   b. Are they ready to move quickly in any direction to intercept Wolves?
   c. Do they keep Wolves and Sheep apart without touching, pushing, or roughing Wolves?

2. Do Wolves feint and move quickly to outmaneuver their guards?

3. Does each Sheep consider the total situation in planning his own strategy for reaching the fold safely?

4. Does each child have the endurance to complete the game without undue fatigue?

NOTES

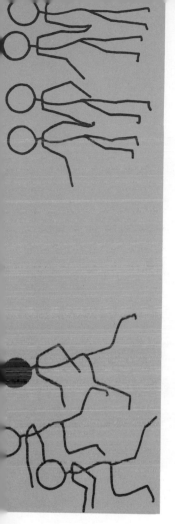

in
Space

Players:
9–15 per group

Equipment:
none

Behavioral goal: To run swiftly and avoid a chaser while meeting a partner; to overtake and tag an opponent

Children who are Space Ships line up in pairs, facing child who is the Enemy Interceptor, standing with his back toward the others, eyes straight ahead. When Interceptor calls, "Rendezvous!" the pair at the end of the line run to the front and try to join hands before the Interceptor tags either of them.

If one Space Ship is tagged, the chaser takes the other partner and they take their places at the head of the line. Child who was tagged is the new Enemy Interceptor.

If the chaser is not successful he continues to be IT and Space Ships who successfully completed the rendezvous go to the head of the line.

EVALUATIVE CHECK LIST

1. Is each child ready to move quickly on the signal?

2. Do partners cooperate with each other in outmaneuvering the chaser?

3. Are children able to dodge and change direction quickly?

a. Do they shift weight to foot away from direction of movement, freeing other foot to step in the new direction?

b. Do they lower the center of gravity for a stronger push-off when changing direction?

NOTES

in
Place

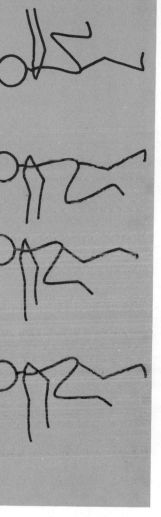

Players:
any number

Equipment:
stopwatch

Behavioral goal: To run in place for increasingly longer periods of time.

On signal, "Run!" children run in place, continuing for as
long as possible. Teacher may use a watch to time the
running, calling off every 15 seconds. When a child
stops, his score is the last 15-second interval called.

Running should be done with the knees lifted as high
as possible, touching the hands, which are held level
with the elbows. Rate of running should be 70–80 steps
per minute. Individual scores should be recorded so each
child can attempt to better his own record.

EVALUATIVE CHECK LIST

1. Does each child understand how running for a longer period each time can improve his endurance? Does he understand how it:

  a. Strengthens the heart muscle by causing it to work harder?

  b. Improves circulation as more blood is pumped to the tissues?

  c. Forces lungs to breathe deeper to get the needed oxygen for the body?

  d. Helps him keep running longer without getting tired?

2. Does each child work on improving his own score rather than competing with others in the class?

NOTES

the
Can

Players:
6–8 per group

Equipment:
1 can per group

Behavioral goal: To overtake and tag many runners; to avoid being tagged.

A can is placed in the center of the play area, with a "prison" near by. IT covers his eyes and counts aloud to 10 by ones, as all other children scatter around the play area, staying within the defined boundaries. Upon the count of 10, IT may chase and try to tag any number of players. Those so tagged must go to "prison" where they must remain until completion of the game.

There are no "safe" areas for the runners. If one runner, however, can get close enough to kick the can, all other players are now safe and the game is finished. IT's score is the number of players in prison upon the completion of the game.

IT chooses a new IT and the game continues until each player has had a turn at being IT. The child with the highest score is the group winner.

EVALUATIVE CHECK LIST

1. Does each child have the endurance to keep running until the game is finished?

2. Does each child try to outwit IT and kick the can, thus saving the other runners?

3. Is each child able to change direction quickly to avoid being tagged?

a. Does he center his weight on the foot away from the direction of movement, leaving other foot free to step in the new direction?

b. Does he push off strongly, keeping his weight low?

c. Does he keep feet in stride position to help maintain balance when stopping quickly?

NOTES

Choice

Players:
any number in groups of four

Equipment:
none

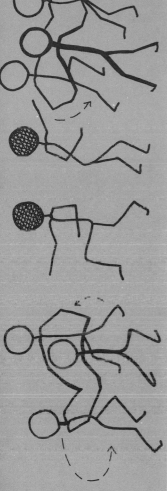

Behavioral goal: To dodge quickly and tag one's choice; to avoid being tagged.

Children are in groups of four, with one child in each group designated as the Monster. The other three children in each group join hands in circles of three, with each Monster on the outside of his own circle. The Monster chooses one child in the circle to tag.

Teacher calls, "Monster's choice!" and all Monsters try to tag their designated choices, while each circle moves to prevent the Monster from tagging the designated child. Monsters may go around one side or the other, but may not go through or over in tagging.

If the designated child is tagged, he becomes the new Monster in his group for the next game. If he is not tagged by the time the teacher calls, "Stop!" the old Monster continues when the new game starts, but chooses another child in the circle to tag.

Variation: Game may end as soon as one Monster tags his choice and becomes winner of the Monsters. New Monsters are chosen in each group until all have been Monster.

EVALUATIVE CHECK LIST

1. Does each child have the endurance to continue moving and dodging until the game is ended?

2. Is each child able to start and stop quickly, shifting weight from side to side as he changes direction in the circle?

    a. Does he keep his center of gravity low by bending his knees?

    b. Does he push off strongly in the new directions?

    c. Does he coordinate his movement with the other two circle players?

3. Does each child maintain his emotional control during the heat of the game?

    a. Does he accept physical discomfort in good fellowship?

    b. Does he accept defeat when tagged without feeling that the group "let him down"?

    c. Does he cooperate with other circle players to prevent them from being tagged?

NOTES

Tag

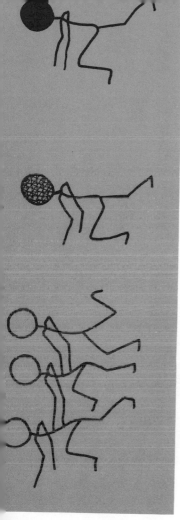

Players:
6–8 groups of three

Equipment:
none

Behavioral goal: To dodge in unison with two others; to move quickly to tag another.

Children scatter around the play area in groups of three, the players in each group in single file behind each other. Each has his hands around the waist of the one in front. The third child in line is the Bronco's Tail, the first is the Head, and the second the Body.

Two children are the runner and the chaser. To save himself from being tagged, the runner must catch hold of a Bronco's Tail. If the runner succeeds, the Head of the Bronco becomes the new runner. The Bronco tries to keep his Tail from being tagged by dodging around to keep it out of reach of the runner.

If the chaser tags the runner before he can catch a Bronco's Tail, the runner becomes the chaser.

EVALUATIVE CHECK LIST

1. Does each child have the endurance to continue running until he fulfills his role in the game?

2. Is each child able to dodge and change direction quickly?
   a. Does he shift weight to the foot away from direction of movement, freeing other foot to step in the new direction?
   b. Does he lower his center of gravity for a stronger push-off?

3. Do children cooperate with each other in saving the Tail of the Bronco from being tagged?
   a. Do they hold tightly to the player in front?
   b. Do they move quickly in unison with others?

NOTES

for
Distance

Players:
any number

Equipment:
none

Behavioral goal: To walk-run as far and as long as possible.

A circular course is marked out around the play area and is divided into quarters for scoring purposes. Children start at the starting line and walk 10 steps, then run 10 steps, continuing to walk-run for as many laps as possible. The child's score is the number of quarters he completes without stopping.

Each child may have a partner who scores for him, and he in turn scores for his partner; thus, half of the class may run at one time. Individual rather than group scores should be emphasized, with each child trying to better his score from day to day.

EVALUATIVE CHECK LIST

1. Does each child understand what endurance is and the conditions that affect it?

a. Muscular aspect? (Stronger muscles have greater endurance.)

b. Circulo-respiratory aspect? (There is increased efficiency in circulation of blood to tissues and oxygen uptake from inspired air.)

c. Psychological aspect? (Are they willing to accept discomfort of strenuous effort?)

d. Mechanical aspect? (Improved skill of performance will permit the individual to endure for longer time at same energy cost.)

2. Does each child understand how running can improve the circulo-respiratory aspect of endurance? Do they understand how it:

a. Strengthens heart muscle by causing it to work harder?

b. Improves circulation as more blood is pumped to tissues?

c. Forces lungs to breathe deeper to get needed oxygen?

3. Does each child understand how improving his running skill will improve his endurance?

4. Does each child concentrate on improving his own score from day to day rather than competing with others in the class?

NOTES

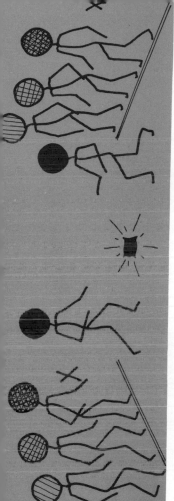

Players:
10–20 per group

Equipment:
1 beanbag or Indian club per group

Behavioral goal: To outmaneuver another player and score a point for one's team by carrying the beanbag over the goal line, or by tagging the opponent.

Children are divided into two equal teams with all players on each team numbered consecutively. Each team stands on its own goal line. A beanbag or Indian club is placed halfway between the goal lines.

Teacher calls a number. The child from each team having that number runs to the beanbag and tries to carry it safely across his own goal line without being tagged by the opposing runner. If a runner carries the beanbag safely to his goal, he scores one point for his team. If he is tagged before crossing the goal, the tagger scores a point for his team.

If either player touches the beanbag or picks it up and drops it, the opposing player can score by tagging him before he reaches the goal. If both players hesitate for a time in picking up the beanbag, the other players may count aloud in unison to 10, upon which both players retire to their own goal lines and no score is recorded for either side.

EVALUATIVE CHECK LIST

1. Does each child understand how to change direction rapidly?

    a. Does he shift weight to the foot away from the direction of movement, freeing the other foot to step in new direction?

    b. Does he lower the center of gravity over the foot carrying weight by bending the knee, then push off strongly in new direction?

2. Does each child understand how to move quickly from a bending or squatting position (when picking up bean-bag) to running?

    a. Does he widen the base of support with feet in stride position?

    b. Does he lean in the direction of movement while pushing off strongly from base?

NOTES

Prison

Flag

Players:
12–20 per group

Equipment:
2 flags per group

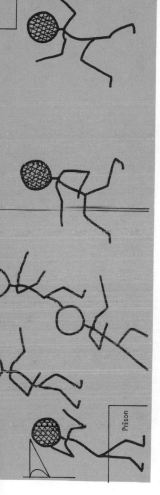

Behavioral goal: To capture the opponents' flag and protect one's own flag from the opponents.

Players are divided into two even teams. Each team has its own court with its own flag on the back line of its court. Each team also has a "prison" marked off in the back part of its court.

Each team tries to capture the opponents' flag and prevent the capture of its own flag. If a player manages to get the opponents' flag and carry it safely into his own court without being tagged, his team wins the game.

If a player is tagged while in enemy territory, he must go into the enemy prison. A teammate may rescue a prisoner by going into the prison, taking his hand, and running home with him. If rescuer and prisoner are tagged while in enemy territory, both become prisoners. Only one prisoner may be rescued at a time, and the rescuer may not take the flag while he is rescuing a prisoner.

EVALUATIVE CHECK LIST

1. Does each child understand how to start quickly by applying force to the best advantage?
   a. Does he lean forward so that force may be applied toward a horizontal direction while reducing vertical movements to a minimum?
   b. Does he push off forcibly from the back foot to overcome inertia and start the body moving?

2. Does each child understand how to stop quickly and change direction?
   a. Does he lower the center of gravity by bending the knees?
   b. Does he shift weight to foot away from direction of movement, then push off strongly in the new direction?

3. Does each team plan strategy cooperatively?

4. Does each child face decisions realistically and accept the results?

NOTES

Prison

Players:
16–20 per group

Equipment:
1 strip of cloth (tail) per person

Behavioral goal: To overtake an opponent and steal his own "tail" while protecting one's own "tail" from thievery.

Children are divided into two or more equal teams. Each team has a goal (safety area) and a prison for captives, with neutral ground between the goals. Each player has a "bunny tail" (piece of colored cloth) tucked into the belt at the back. Each team uses tails of the same color to identify its members. Tails may not be tied to the belt.

Players go into neutral ground to steal tails from other teams. When a tail is taken from a player he becomes a prisoner of the person who snatched it and must go to that team's prison.

The team that captures all the opponents, or who has the most prisoners at the end of the given playing time, is the winner.

EVALUATIVE CHECK LIST

1. Does each child have the endurance to keep moving and dodging until the game is ended?

2. Is each child able to start, stop, and change direction quickly and effetively?

3. Is each child able to accept loss of his "tail" objectively, rather than taking personal issue with the captor?

4. Do team members work together constructively?
   a. Do they plan how to protect each other as they try to snatch opponents' tails?
   b. Do they plan strategy in drawing opponents into neutral ground?

5. Are children able to avoid developing or carrying over animosities toward opponents?

NOTES

RELAYS AND RACES

gen and carbon dioxide to and from the muscles. Relays and races may contribute to the development of endurance if the child moves rapidly enough for a long enough time to place stress upon his cardiovascular system, that is, to become "out of breath."

Any type of locomotor movement lends itself to relays and races. These activities are frequently used at parties and other recreational events and are fun for both adults and children. Relays and races use many movement skills. In addition to the specific mode of locomotion (walking, running, hopping, and the like) these activities emphasize starting quickly, stopping, and frequently changing direction, as in the shuttle races.

To perform the standing start, the child stands with feet in a stride position with one foot near the starting line. He leans forward, with knees "easy." At the signal, "On your marks!" the runner is alert, with head up and elbows bent. On "Get set!" the child leans forward, with much of his weight on the forward foot, and on "Go!" he pushes off with the forward foot as the back foot swings forward to receive

Relays and races involve moving quickly from one place to another, either individually or as team members. The child may race against time, his score being the number of seconds it takes him to move a given distance, or he may race against another child or children.

Endurance is dependent upon the ability of the

the weight. The body leans forward for the first few steps, which are short and quick, and the stride lengthens as the runner moves at top speed with knees bent and elbows flexed.

Race

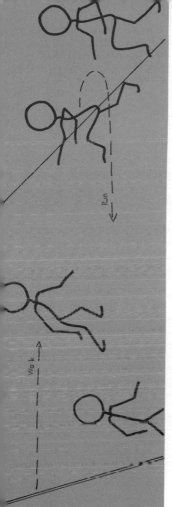

Players:
any number

Equipment:
none

Behavioral goal: To walk quickly and run fast in racing others.

Children line up side by side on the starting line. On signal "Go!" they walk rapidly to the opposite line, then turn and run back to the starting line. Winner is the first child to return to the starting line.

To develop endurance the racing distance may be gradually increased.

Suggested variations:

1. *Crawl-run Race: crawling on hands and knees to opposite line and running back;*
2. *Skip-run Race;*
3. *Hop-run Race;*
4. *Backward-forward Race: walking backward to the opposite line and walking (or running) forward on return trip.*

EVALUATIVE CHECK LIST

1. Does each child understand how to improve his racing time?

   a. Is he prepared to push off immediately on signal "Go!"?

   b. Does he keep going as fast as possible until *after* crossing finish line, slowing down *after* crossing finish line?

2. Does each child understand how to improve his endurance through running?

   a. Does he run a greater distance each day?

   b. Does he run faster each day?

3. Does each child have the courage to finish the race, even if he sees he is not winning?

NOTES

Race

Players:
any number

Equipment:
none

Behavioral goal: To bear-walk from one line to another as quickly as possible.

Children line up in back of starting line. On signal "Go" they bear-walk to finish line. First player to reach finish line is the winner.

Note: to do the bear-walk, children get down on all fours and walk on hands and feet.

Variations:

1. *Bunny Hop:* squatting and folding arms around knees and hopping in this position;

2. *Elephant Walk:* with body bent forward and arms swinging like a trunk;

3. *Wild Horse Gallop;*

4. *Crab Walk:* squatting and reaching backward until hands are on ground; walking on heels and palms with back parallel to floor;

5. *Bird Race:* "flying" to opposite line;

6. *Caterpillar Race:* inching along like a caterpillar;

7. *Kangaroo Hop:* holding an object such as a piece of paper or a beanbag between knees and jumping with feet together.

EVALUATIVE CHECK LIST

1. Does each child perform the bear walk correctly, using both hands and feet as he moves?

2. Does each child start immediately on signal "Go!" and continue until he crosses the finish line?

NOTES

Home
the
Beanbag

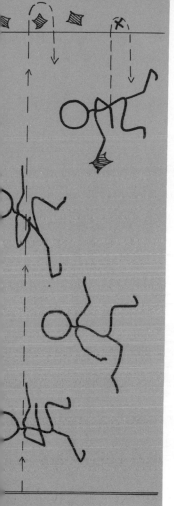

Players:
any number

Equipment:
1 beanbag per player

Behavioral goal: To retrieve an object and carry it back across the line as fast as possible.

Children line up side by side on the starting line. A beanbag is placed opposite each runner on a line 20–30 feet away from and parallel to the starting line.

On signal "Go!" runners run to their beanbags, each runner picking up his own beanbag and carrying it back across the starting line. The first runner to cross the line with the beanbag in his possession is the winner.

Suggested variations:

1. *Carry home the valentine;*
2. *Carry home the toy;*
3. *Carry home the Easter egg;*
4. *Carry home the Christmas tree;*
5. *Carry home the Jack-o-lantern;*
6. *Carry home the turkey;*
7. *Carry home any other holiday or storybook character.*

EVALUATIVE CHECK LIST

1. Does each child know how to improve his racing time?
   a. Does he lean forward and push off immediately on signal?
   b. Does he keep going at top speed across finish line?
   c. Does he improve his running by pushing off forcefully, landing on balls of feet, knees easy, arms swinging easily?

2. Does each child understand how to improve his endurance by running?
   a. Does he run a greater distance on consecutive days?
   b. Does he run faster each time?

3. Does each child try to give his best performance, even though he may not win the race?

4. Are children good winners and good losers?
   a. Do they recognize improvement in others?
   b. Do they avoid ridiculing the performance of others?
   c. Do they have the courage to finish the race, even though losing?

NOTES

Race

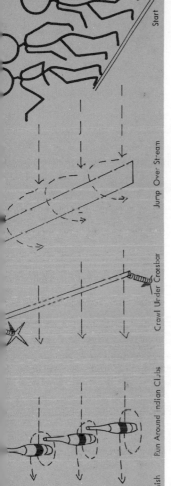

Finish   Run Around Indian Clubs   Crawl Under Crossbar   Jump Over Stream   Start

Players:
any number

Equipment:
various obstacles, such as apparatus, boxes, Indian clubs

Behavioral goal: To perform the various challenges as quickly as possible.

This race provides various challenges or obstacles to be overcome. Children line up at the starting line. On the signal "Go!" they try to reach the finish line as fast as possible, overcoming each obstacle in the pathway to the finish line.

The obstacles are a "stream" to be jumped or leaped over (two parallel lines marked 2–3 feet apart), a bar to be crawled under (high jump standards with pole across), and an Indian club to be circled. First child to reach the finish line after performing the challenges correctly is the winner.

Other obstacles to be overcome:

1. Go over and through a row of barrels or boxes;
2. Go over or through or around favorite pieces of playground apparatus;
3. Walk a balance beam or chalk line;
4. Perform stunts at various stations, such as a sit-up at one place, a push-up at another, a forward roll at another, and so on.

EVALUATIVE CHECK LIST

1. Does each child know how to improve his racing time?
   a. Does he start immediately on signal?
   b. Does he practice performing the various challenges until he is proficient?
   c. Does he keep going at top speed across finish line?

2. Does each child understand how to improve his endurance by running the challenge course?
   a. Does he run for a longer time each day?
   b. Does he run faster each day?

NOTES

Zoo Race

Players:
20–30

Equipment:
none

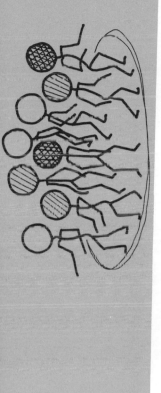

Behavioral goal: To race home from the "zoo" as fast as possible.

Children are divided into three or four groups. Each group takes the name of a zoo animal, and all stand within the boundaries of a designated area (the zoo).

On the signal "Go!" they break out of their "cages" and run to their homes in the "forest." The winning group is the one in which all "animals" of the group reach "home" before all animals of the other groups.

Suggested variations:

1. *Toy Race: children take names of toys;*
2. *Bird Race: children take bird names;*
3. *Halloween Race: Halloween characters are chosen.*

EVALUATIVE CHECK LIST

1. Does each player know what he is to do, and can he do it without coaching from others?

2. Is each child able to avoid collisions with others as he runs rapidly to the designated "home"?

3. Is each child able to start quickly on the signal?

NOTES

Needle

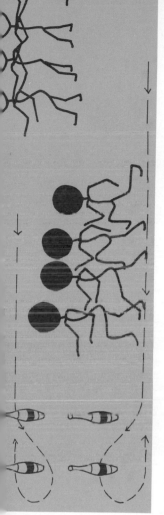

Players:
any number

Equipment:
2 Indian clubs per group of five or six

Behavioral goal: To run fast while staying in formation with other team members.

Children line up in groups of five or six. Each group lines up in file formation on the starting line with hands on shoulders of teammate in front. This line of players is the "thread."

An Indian club is on the ground about 40 feet in front of each team, with a second Indian club placed 2 feet beyond the first (see illustration). The space between the two clubs is the "eye" of the needle. On signal "Go," children drop hands and staying in their positions in line, they run between the Indian clubs through the eye of the needle and back to their starting positions, ending with hands on the shoulders of the player in front.

The team first back into the original starting position is the winner, if the team members have stayed in line while running. If a team member knocks over an Indian club, it must be replaced immediately before the team can continue threading the needle.

Suggested variations:

1. Train Race: trains make a straight run from one position to another, or a circular or figure eight run;

2. "Santa's reindeer" pull Santa in his sleigh, with eight children as reindeer and one child at end of line as Santa;

3. Centipede Race: each child is a leg of the centipede.

EVALUATIVE CHECK LIST

1. Does each child stay in his position in line?
   a. Does he avoid running out of line or passing players?
   b. Does he move rapidly enough to keep up with the player ahead of him?

2. Does each child have the endurance needed to complete the race efficiently?

3. Does each team accept the limitations of its members and help them to succeed?
   a. Do teammates encourage each other?
   b. Do they avoid harsh comments toward slower runners?

NOTES

Line Race

Players:
any number

Equipment:
none

Behavioral goal: To race an opponent and win a point for one's team

The players are divided into teams of six to eight members. Each team lines up on the starting line, standing in file formation, each person in back of the other. On the signal "Go!" the first player in each team runs to the opposite line, touches it with his foot, and runs back across the starting line. The first player back is the winner of the race and scores 1 point for his team.

On the signal "Go!" the second players on each team run and the winner is determined. This continues until all have run. The team with the most points is the winner.

Note: When children become adept in this team racing, they may run the race in relay formation, with each child touching off the next runner in his team as he returns.

EVALUATIVE CHECK LIST

1. Does each child know how to improve his racing time?

   a. Does he lean forward and push off immediately on signal?

   b. Does he keep going at top speed across the finish line?

2. Does each child know how to change direction quickly?

   a. Does he shift weight to the foot that is away from the direction of movement, freeing the opposite foot to step in the new direction?

   b. Does he lower the center of gravity by bending the knees, providing a stronger push-off toward the new direction?

3. Does each child have the endurance to complete the race efficiently?

4. Does each team accept limitations of its members and help them to succeed?

   a. Does it encourage team members?

   b. Do players avoid harsh and derogatory comments?

NOTES

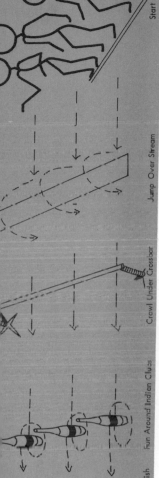

Players:
any number

Equipment:
various obstacles

Behavioral goal: To perform the various challenges in sequence as quickly as possible.

Finish   Run Around Indian Clubs   Crawl Under Crossbar   Jump Over Stream   Start

Children line up at starting line. On Signal "Go!" they try to reach the finish line as fast as possible, overcoming each obstacle in the pathway to the finish line. The obstacles may be a stream to be leaped over, a bar to be crawled under, and an Indian club to be circled. The first child to reach the finish line after performing the challenges correctly is the winner.

Other obstacles to be overcome may be boxes and barrels to go over and through; various types of play-ground apparatus to climb over or crawl through; a balance beam to walk; stunts to perform, such as forward roll; and the like.

Relays and Races: grades 1, 2   **129**

EVALUATIVE CHECK LIST

1. Does each child know how to improve his racing time?
   a. Does he start immediately on signal?
   b. Does he practice performing the various challenges until he is proficient?
   c. Does he keep going at top speed across the finish line?

2. Does each child understand how to improve his endurance running the challenge course?
   a. Does he run for a longer time each day?
   b. Does he run faster each day?

NOTES

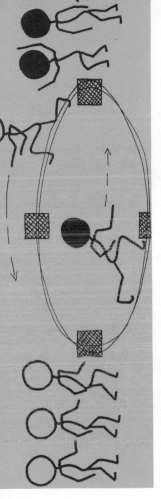

the
Bases

Players:
any number

Equipment:
first, second, third and fourth bases

Behavioral goal: To run fast and circle the bases, trying to defeat the other team.

Children divide into two teams. One team lines up in single file behind first base and the other team behind third base (see illustration). On signal "Go!" the first player of each team circles the bases, tagging each base with his foot as he passes it. When he returns to his team he touches the next player in line, who circles the bases.

The team that first gets all players back into original positions is the winner.

EVALUATIVE CHECK LIST

1. Does each child have the endurance to run the bases rapidly without stopping?

2. Does each child understand how endurance can be improved by running a greater distance each time, or by running faster each time?
   a. Does he increase the distance between bases?
   b. Does he run the bases twice without stopping?

3. Does each child know how to improve his running?
   a. Does he start immediately on signal?
   b. Does he push off from the back foot?
   c. Does he land on balls of feet, knees easy?
   d. Does he avoid losing momentum by tagging base without stopping?

NOTES

Race

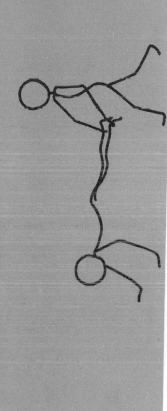

Players:
any number of twos

Equipment:
none

Behavioral goal: To cooperate with a partner in racing others.

Children divide into teams of four to six couples. Teams line up in back of starting line, each couple forming a "wheelbarrow." On signal "Go!" the first wheelbarrow in each team races to the opposite line and returns, touching off the next wheelbarrow, continuing until all wheelbarrows have raced. Winner is team who finishes first.

"Wheelbarrow" is formed by one child getting down on all fours while his partner grasps ankles, raising feet and legs off the floor (see illustration). Children move forward, the first child walking on his hands as his partner supports his legs.

The racing distance should be determined by the strength and abilities of the children, starting with a short distance of several feet and gradually increasing the distance as the children gain in strength.

EVALUATIVE CHECK LIST

1. Does each child have the arm and shoulder strength to move quickly on the hands while his feet are supported by a partner?

2. Do children cooperate with each other in moving quickly while the body is in an unusual position?

   a. Does the child who supports his partner's legs coordinate his speed with his partner's?

   b. Is the supporting child careful not to push his partner on his face?

3. Does each child accept the discomfort of trying to move in an awkward position?

   a. Does he accept the challenge of walking on his hands as the "wheelbarrow"?

   b. Does he make an effort to move his fastest?

NOTES

Reptiles
Relay

Players:
any number

Equipment:
none

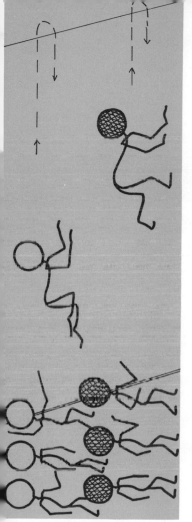

Behavioral goal: To run fast while imitating the movement of a reptile.

Children divide into even teams of four to six players per team. Teams line up on starting lines in file formation. Each team member imitates a predetermined reptile as he races to the opposite line and returns, touching off the next runner in his team.

For example, all number 1 runners in each team may be alligators, number 2 runners may be iguanas, number 3 runners may be dinosaurs, number 4 runners may be geckos, and so on. First runners in line start on signal. "Go!" and run to opposite line, return, and touch next runner in line. Team that finishes first is winner.

Suggested variations:

1. Jungle Animals Relay: children imitate lions, tigers, giraffes, elephants, monkeys, and the like;

2. Farm Animals Relay: children are cows, horses, pigs, ducks, sheep, and so on;

3. Space Animals Relay: children imitating imaginary space animals (space birds, hopping and cackling; space dragons; and so on).

Relays and Races: grades 3, 4   135

EVALUATIVE CHECK LIST

1. Are children imaginative in trying to move in the pattern of the animal they are imitating?

2. Does each child have the strength to move quickly with his body in an unusual position?

3. Does each child have the endurance needed to complete the race?

4. Do children accept the limitations of each team member and help everyone feel successful and confident?

NOTES

Relay

Players' Line

Leaders' Line

Players:
any number

Equipment:
none

Behavioral goal: To run fast with a partner.

Players divide into even teams. Each team has a leader who stands on the "leaders' line" facing other teammates, who are lined up in file formation on the "players' line" (see illustration).

On signal "Go!" leader runs to first player on his team, takes his hand and runs with him back to the leaders' line. The leader remains on this line, and the rescued player runs back to the team and brings the next player to the leaders' line with him. This continues until all are rescued.

Team who first gets all players behind the leaders' line is the winner.

EVALUATIVE CHECK LIST

1. Does each child understand how to start and stop quickly?

   a. Does he lean forward and start immediately on signal?

   b. Does he bend knees to lower his center of gravity and spread the feet to widen the base of support, to stop quickly?

2. Are children able to run successfully with a partner?

   a. Can they adjust speed to the other person?

   b. Do they encourage each other to maximum effort?

3. Does each child have the endurance to complete the race at top speed?

4. Do children plan how to arrange teams that will be nearly equal in ability, to make the race more enjoyable?

   a. Is the group objective in evaluating the running abilities of its members?

   b. Is each child realistic in assessing his own running ability and plan with the group how to set up "fair" teams?

NOTES

Relay

Players:
any number

Equipment:
none

Behavioral goal: To run fast and help win the relay.

Children divide into even teams, 5–10 players per team. Half of each team faces the other half (see illustration).

On signal "Go!" the first player on the starting line runs and touches off the first player on the opposite line and goes to the end of that line. The player touched off runs to the starting line and touches off the next player in that line, then goes to the end of that line. This continues until both halves are back in their original positions.

The team that gets all of its players back to the original positions first is the winner.

EVALUATIVE CHECK LIST

1. Does each child know how to achieve his best running speed?

   a. Does he lean forward and start immediately on signal?
   b. Does he run full speed across the finish line, tagging the next player as he passes him?
   c. Does he improve his running skill?
   d. Does he improve his endurance?

2. Does each child have the opportunity to improve his running skill?

   a. Does he receive assistance in analyzing his own running?
   b. Is he given opportunities for practice?

3. Is each player able to perform skillfully under stress?

   a. Does he start at the correct time?
   b. Does he touch off the next runner properly?
   c. Does he go to end of line?
   d. Is he ready to run again?

NOTES

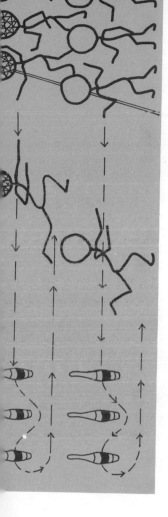

Light Relay

Players:
any number

Equipment:
3 Indian clubs per team

Behavioral goal: To run fast and help one's team win the relay.

Children divide into even teams, 6–10 per team. Each team stands in file formation behind the starting line. Three Indian clubs or beanbags are placed in line with each team, 30 feet from the starting line and 5 feet apart.

On the signal "Go!" the first player in each team runs to his team's clubs, and going to the right of the first club, he weaves through them in a figure eight. Then he weaves back and touches off the next runner.

The team that first gets back to the original lineup is the winner.

1. Are children able to weave rapidly around the clubs without losing balance?

   a. Do they carry body weight forward?

   b. Do they lean toward the clubs?

   c. Do they lower the center of gravity by bending the knees, providing a stronger push-off toward the new direction?

   d. Do they keep moving to avoid losing momentum?

2. Does each child have the endurance to complete his race at top speed?

3. Do team members encourage each other?

   a. Do they avoid destructive comments or ridicule?

   b. Do they help the runner feel confident of his ability to succeed?

   c. Do they graciously accept either winning or losing?

NOTES

Course Race

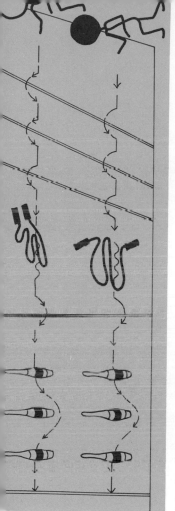

Players:
any number

Equipment:
obstacles, such as apparatus, ropes, hurdles, and so on

Behavioral goal: To perform the various challenges in appropriate sequence, moving as quickly as possible.

Children line up at starting line. On signal "Go!" they try to reach the finish line as fast as possible, overcoming each obstacle in the path on the way to the finish line.

The obstacles are three hurdles to be leaped over; a rope to be jumped over three times; a bar to be crawled under; three Indian clubs to weave through; and, finally, the child hops to the finish line.

Other challenge courses may be set up, using any obstacles available, such as old automobile tires to step into, ropes to climb, boxes or horses to vault or climb over, mazes to run through, and so on.

Relays and Races: grades 3, 4   143

EVALUATIVE CHECK LIST

1. Does each child have the confidence to attempt each challenge?

2. Does each child know how to improve his ability to run the challenge course?

   a. Does he start immediately on signal?

   b. Does he practice performing the various challenges until he is proficient?

   c. Does he keep going at top speed across the finish line?

3. Does each child have the strength and endurance to perform the various challenges and to continue until he has finished the course?

4. Does each child understand how to improve his biologic efficiency in running the challenge course?

   a. Does he try to improve his speed in performance of the various challenges?

   b. Does he perform additional challenges each day?

NOTES

the World

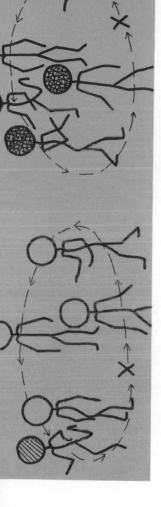

Players:
any number

Equipment:
none

Behavioral goal: To run rapidly around the circle, defeating an opponent.

Children divide into even teams; each team stands in a circle facing the center. Each team member is given a number in consecutive order, beginning with number 1.

The teacher calls a number and the players with this number run around outside of their respective circles and back to place. The player who arrives first is winner and scores 1 point for his team. The team that first scores 11 points is the winner (or the team with the most points after all have run is the winner).

Variation: This game may be played as a relay, with all number 1's completing the circle, then touching off the next player in the circle until all have run once.

EVALUATIVE CHECK LIST

1. Is each child able to run rapidly in a circle?
   a. Does he lean toward center of circle?
   b. Does he avoid touching or holding other circle players as he runs?
   c. Does he keep moving, thus taking advantage of momentum?

2. Is each player ready to move quickly when his number is called?

3. Does each child have the endurance to run swiftly around the circle without undue fatigue?

NOTES

Relay

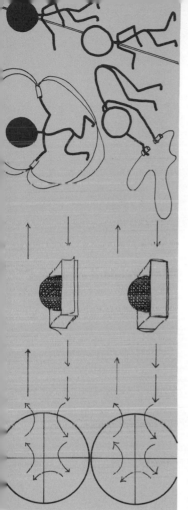

Players:
any number

Equipment:
1 jump rope, box, and ball per team

Behavioral goal: To overcome the various obstacles as quickly as possible.

Children divide into even teams and line up single file on the starting line. Thirty feet from the starting line a circle is drawn for each team and a jump rope is placed inside it. Ten feet from the circle is a box with a rubber ball in it, and 10 feet from the box is a circle, which is quartered and numbered from 1 to 4 (see illustration).

On signal "Go!" the first player in each team runs to the first circle and picks up the rope, jumping it once and replacing it; then runs to the box, removes the ball, bounces it three times, and replaces it in the box; then

runs to the final circle and hops into 1, then into 2, 3, and 4. Player then runs back to his team and touches the next player in line, who in turn, runs the obstacles. This continues until all team members have run. The winner is the team finishing first.

Variations: Other obstacles may be used, such as playground apparatus to climb over or crawl through, hurdles or bars to jump, horizontal ladders to walk, mazes to run through, stunts to perform, and so on.

EVALUATIVE CHECK LIST

1. Is each child able to perform the various challenges?

   a. Does he have the strength and endurance to perform successfully?

   b. Does he have the coordination and flexibility to perform successfully?

2. Does each child have the confidence to attempt each challenge?

3. Does each child understand how to improve his biologic efficiency in running the challenge course?

   a. Does he practice the various challenges until he is proficient in execution?

   b. Does he try to improve his speed in performance of the various challenges?

   c. Does he perform additional challenges each day?

NOTES

Race

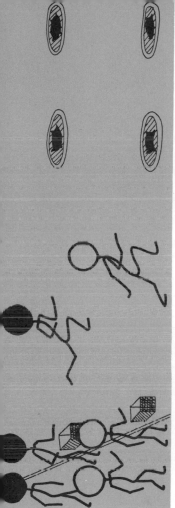

Players:
any number

Equipment:
3 boxes and 2 beanbags per team

Behavioral goal: To retrieve potatoes and replace them while moving as fast as possible.

Children divide into even teams and line up single file behind the starting line. A box, base, or circle may be used as a container for the potatoes (beanbags or blocks of wood). The distance from the starting line to the first potato is 24 feet; the second potato is placed 8 feet from the first potato (see illustration). A box is also placed on starting line.

On signal "Go!" the first player on each team retrieves either potato and places it in the box on the starting line. Then he gets the other potato and touches the box on the starting line with it, then returns the potato to its original position. He returns to the box on the starting line, gets the potato from it, and returns it to its original position. Then he runs back to the starting line and touches off the next runner, who continues the process. Potatoes may be taken and replaced by each runner in turn in any order the runner chooses.

Team finishing first is the winner.

EVALUATIVE CHECK LIST

1. Does each child have the endurance needed to finish the race without undue fatigue?

2. Is each child able to maintain equilibrium while picking up objects and changing direction quickly?

3. Is each child able to perform skillfully under stress?
   a. Does he start at correct time?
   b. Does he perform the sequence of events correctly?
   c. Does he touch off teammate properly?

NOTES

Jump the Stick Relay

Players:
any number

Equipment:
1 long wand per team

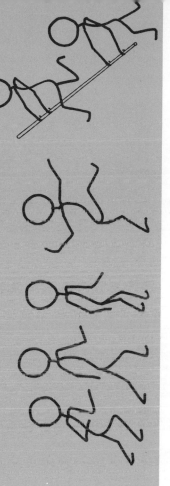

Behavioral goal: To jump the stick skillfully when it is placed under one's feet; to carry the stick in turn.

Children divide into even teams with team members in file formation. Teams should stand about 10 feet apart. First player in each team holds a stick or wand. On the signal "Go!" the first player hands the other end of the wand to the second player in line, and holding it between them they run the length of their line, dragging the stick under the feet of their teammates. Players in line jump over the stick as it reaches their feet.

When the players with the stick reach the end of the line, the first player lets go of the stick and stays at the end of the line. The second player runs back to the head of the line with the stick and hands the other end to the number 3 player. These two run down the line as before. This continues until player number 1 is back in his original position at the head of the line.

The team to finish first is the winner.

EVALUATIVE CHECK LIST

1. Does each child have the endurance to finish the relay without undue fatigue?

2. Is each child able to perform skillfully under stress?
   a. Does he understand what he is to do and move to do it at the proper time?
   b. Does he avoid hitting or tripping players with the wand?
   c. Is he alert in jumping over the wand at the proper time?

NOTES

activities need no equipment and may be performed in the classroom or on the play field. Others use specific types of equipment and special surfaces for landing, rebounding balls, and the like.

The stunts suggested for younger children involve the use of the body in different positions, with and without apparatus. Six and seven year olds are capable of twisting their bodies into many different positions because their joints are flexible enough to permit a wide range of movement. Their shorter legs place the center of gravity near the base of support, giving them good stability in balancing activities. This is the golden age of childhood for exploring and experimenting, and experiencing many different body positions and movement skills.

Many activities suggested for younger children may also challenge older children. It is not practical to state the absolute degree of difficulty of any stunt, since much depends upon the body structure, development, attitude, and previous experiences of the individual attempting the stunt. Grade levels are designated to help the teacher make a selection for a particular group, but it must be remembered that any

STUNTS AND TESTS

Stunts and tests measure performance of basic movements of the body involving equilibrium or balance, use of levers, range of motion in joints, and various physiologic factors such as strength, endurance, flexibility, coordination, and agility.

Some of these activities may be performed by one individual working alone, others require a partner, and still others are designed for a group of individ-

activities may be suitable for any grade level and may even be challenging to adults.

Stunts and tests provide useful opportunities for helping the growing child adapt to the demands of a changing body; such adaptation is one of the developmental tasks of late childhood.

Rope Walker

Players:
4–6 per group

Equipment:
balance beam

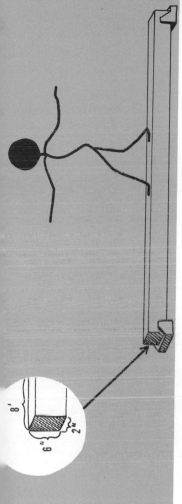

Behavioral goal: To perform stunts on the "tight rope."

Children walk on a balance beam, or a line drawn on the floor, in the following ways:

1. Do heel-toe walk forward, placing the heel of one foot at the toes of the other;
2. Take giant steps (long steps forward);
3. Take baby steps (short steps forward);
4. Balance on two feet for a count of 5;
5. Balance on one foot for a count of 5;
6. Walk backward on the beam;
7. Walk sideward on the beam;
8. Make up your own stunts for the beam.

The balance beam may be approximately 8–10 inches from the floor, for safety in case the child should lose balance. Before walking on the beam, children may first

Stunts and Tests: Kindergarten   155

try walking on a line on the floor. Arms may be extended from the sides to help in balancing the body.

Children may invent other stunts to do on the beam, using different locomotor patterns, changing direction and level.

EVALUATIVE CHECK LIST

1. Does each child know how to maintain balance on the beam?
   a. Does he wear clean tennis shoes on a clean plank?
   b. Does he keep his weight centered over his feet?
   c. Does he bend his knees?
   d. Does he spread his feet apart?

2. Do children help each other?
   a. Do they avoid ridicule or laughter if a performer is having difficulty?
   b. Do they give generous approval for a good attempt?

3. Does each child have the courage to try each stunt?

NOTES

the
Head

Players:
6–8 per group

Equipment:
mats

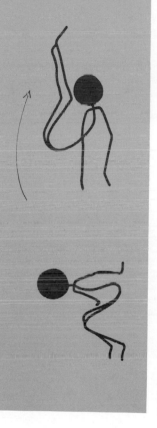

Behavioral goal: To roll backward, touching feet to floor over head.

Child sits on the mat, knees bent, arms at sides. He pushes with his feet, rolling backward and swinging his legs over his head to touch the floor behind his head with his toes.

Variation: Start from a lying position, knees bent and feet on the floor.

EVALUATIVE CHECK LIST

1. Does each child understand that flexibility means range of movement in the joints of the body?

2. Does each child understand how to increase flexibility by stretching in a slow, controlled manner?

3. If unable to touch feet to floor over head, does each child know how to work toward solving the problem?
   a. Can he reach toward the floor with his feet, moving slowly and trying to move a little farther each time?
   b. Does he practice the stunt daily, stretching slowly and a little farther each time?

4. Do children follow safety rules?
   a. Do they perform the stunt on a mat?
   b. Do they avoid interfering with other performers?

NOTES

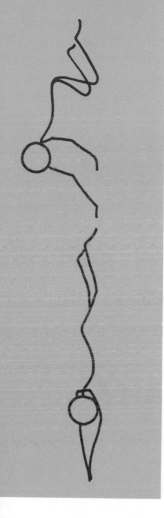

Players:
6–8 per group

Equipment:
mats

Behavioral goal: To "squash" on the mat from a hand-knee position.

Children kneel on mats on hands and knees. On signal "Squash!" they fall forward by extending arms forward and legs backward at the same time. Child should keep his head up to avoid hitting his face or chin. If he relaxes and "gives" with the fall he will not receive as great a shock when his body hits the mat.

EVALUATIVE CHECK LIST

1. Is child able to coordinate arms and legs and squash on the mat?

2. Is child able to relax and "give" with the fall?

3. Do children follow safety rules?

a. Do they keep heads up when falling, to avoid hitting face or chin?

b. Do they await their turns without interfering with other performers?

NOTES

Worm

Players:
any number

Equipment:
none

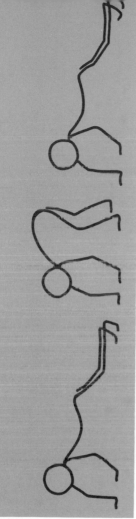

Behavioral goal: To walk like a worm, alternating hands and feet.

Child gets on all fours, putting weight on hands and feet. He walks forward on his hands, keeping his feet stationary until his body is in a straight line. Then flexing his hips, he walks his feet up to his hands. He continues, alternating hands and feet, for as long as possible. Child should keep knees and elbows straight throughout the entire walk.

Variations:

1. Seal Walk: walk forward on hands, dragging legs and toes, back straight and head up. Hips may swing as child moves.

2. Bear Walk: walk on all fours.

3. Crab Walk: sit on floor, lift weight on hands and feet with body facing upward, and walk forward.

4. Angry Cat Walk: walk on all fours, legs straight as possible and back arched.

5. Mule Kick: walk forward on all fours, then stop and kick both feet into air, supporting weight on hands.

EVALUATIVE CHECK LIST

1. Does each child have the strength and flexibility to perform the stunt?

2. Does each child understand how to increase flexibility?
   a. Does he stretch in a slow, controlled manner, moving a little farther each time?
   b. Does he practice stretching daily until desired flexibility is attained?

   c. Does he continue the activities in order to maintain flexibility?

3. Does each child understand how to increase strength?
   a. Does he increase the number of repetitions of the exercise?
   b. Does he increase the rate of exercise?

NOTES

Roll

Players:
4–6 per group

Equipment:
mats

Behavioral goal: To do a somersault, rolling forward with the body curled.

Child squats facing the mat, feet apart and toes touching the mat. He places his hands on the mat just ahead of his toes. He bends his head forward, locking between his legs, and keeping his body curled he pushes with his hands and feet. As he rolls forward he transfers his weight from feet to shoulders and rolls to a sitting position on the mat. The top of his head *never touches the mat.*

Variations:

1. *Roll to a sitting position with feet together.*
2. *Cross feet in midair and roll to sitting position.*
3. *Roll to standing position, giving a push on the mat with hands as weight rolls over feet.*

54

EVALUATIVE CHECK LIST

1. Can each child perform the stunt successfully?
   a. Can he avoid touching his head?
   b. Can he roll from feet to shoulders?
   c. Can he land in sitting or standing position?

2. Does each child understand that to roll successfully he must lose balance?
   a. Does he keep body curled in a ball?
   b. Does he push body off balance with feet?

   c. Does he use momentum to keep rolling to sitting position?

3. Does each child have the courage to attempt the stunt?

4. Do children cooperate with each other?
   a. Do they avoid interfering with the performer in any way?
   b. Do they give helpful suggestions if needed?

NOTES

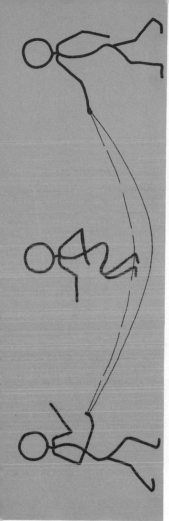

Players:
6–8 per group

Equipment:
one 18–20 foot jumping rope per group

Behavioral goal: To jump over the rope and complete the chant, thus becoming a rope turner.

A rope is swung slowly back and forth like a pendulum, with one child swinging at either end of the rope. The rope is gradually raised higher and higher as the jumper jumps to the following chant:

Tick-tock, tick-tock,
What's the time by the grandfather clock?
It's one, two, three,

and so on to twelve o'clock, or until the jumper misses.

When a jumper jumps to "twelve o'clock," he runs out and becomes a rope turner. If he misses on a number before twelve he goes to the end of the line and takes his turn again. Only good jumpers may be rope turners. When a jumper takes a turner's place, the turner goes to the end of the line. If a turner becomes tired, he may choose a child to take his place.

EVALUATIVE CHECK LIST

1. Does each child have the coordination to jump the rope several times?

2. Do turners accept their responsibility for turning correctly?

   a. Do they swing the rope slowly back and forth?
   b. Do they raise the rope gradually, so that each child has a chance to succeed?

NOTES

the
Plank

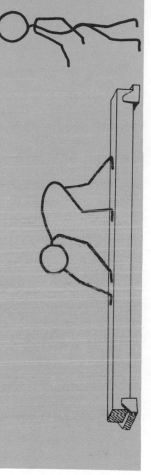

Players:
4–6 per group

Equipment:
balance beam

Behavioral goal: To perform many different stunts on the plank.

Walk on a balance beam, a line drawn on the floor, or a plank placed on the floor, moving in the following ways:

1. *Walk forward on heels, backward on tiptoes.*
2. *Crawl forward, then backward on all fours.*
3. *Walk to center of plank, balance on one foot for count of 3, then walk backward to place.*
4. *Walk to center of plank, kneel on one knee for count of 5, then walk backward to place.*
5. *Walk to center of plank, squat for count of 5, walk backward to place.*
6. *Run on the plank.*
7. *Make up new stunts on the plank.*

Note: If balance beam is not available, a plank 2 inches square and 10 feet long may be used. Tape it to the floor to make it more stable.

EVALUATIVE CHECK LIST

1. Does each child understand how balance can be improved?

   a. Does he wear tennis shoes on a clean plank to increase frictional resistance?

   b. Does he place his center of gravity over his feet?

   c. Does he lower his center of gravity by bending his knees?

   d. Does he widen his base of support by spreading his feet?

2. Can each child perform the various stunts without falling?

3. Do children encourage the performer to do his best while they are awaiting their turns on the plank?

   a. Do they avoid derogatory comments or scornful laughter if the performer has difficulty?

   b. Do they give helpful suggestions when necessary?

   c. Do they avoid unflattering comparisons with others?

4. Does each child have the courage to try every stunt?

NOTES

Top

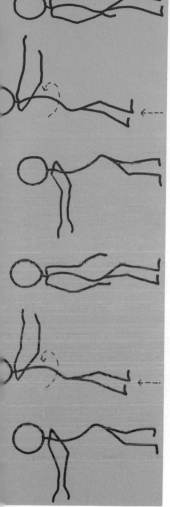

Players:
any number

Equipment:
none

Behavioral goal: To perform a half turn in the air.

Child stands on a line on the floor, feet apart comfortably. He jumps into the air, taking off from both feet, then turns in the air and lands on the line facing the opposite direction from the starting position.

When children perform the half top successfully, they may then try the full top, which is a complete turn in the air with the child landing on the line facing the same direction as in the starting position.

EVALUATIVE CHECK LIST

1. Does each child know how to use force and momentum to help him turn in the air?

   a. Does he bend knees, flex ankles and push against the floor forcibly on take-off?

   b. Does he swing arms and body in the direction of the turn as he leaves the floor?

2. Does each child know how to land without losing balance?

   a. Does he lower the center of gravity by bending knees on landing?

   b. Does he keep the line of gravity over the base of support (back straight, head up)?

   c. Does he spread feet apart for a wider base of support?

3. Does each child know how to lessen the shock of impact on landing?

   a. Does he land on the balls of the feet?

   b. Does he "give" by bending knees and flexing ankles on landing?

NOTES

Rest

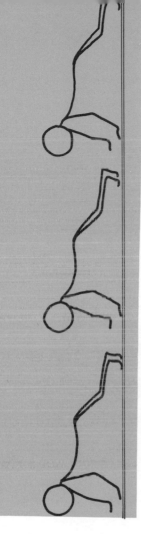

Players:
any number

Equipment:
none

Behavioral goal: To support weight on hands and toes for increasingly longer periods each time.

Child gets down on the floor, supporting his weight on his hands and toes in a squat position. Then he walks his feet backward until there is a straight line from head to toes. His body should not sag at the waist and his hips should not be elevated. He maintains this position for a count of 5. He tries to hold the position for increasingly longer periods on successive days.

Variation: the treadmill: Child takes hand rest position as described above, then keeping hands stationary, he runs in place by alternately bending one leg and extending the other.

EVALUATIVE CHECK LIST

1. Is each child able to support his weight for a minimum count of 5?

2. Does each child understand how this stunt can increase arm strength and endurance? Does he understand that:

   a. If it overloads the muscle it increases strength?

   b. Increasing duration of the exercise improves both strength and endurance as long as it continues to work the muscle harder?

3. Does each child understand how the treadmill exercise will help him increase endurance? Does he understand how it:

   a. Develops heart muscle and improves circulation?

   b. Forces lungs to work harder?

4. Does each child try to improve his own score each day rather than competing with others?

NOTES

Trapeze

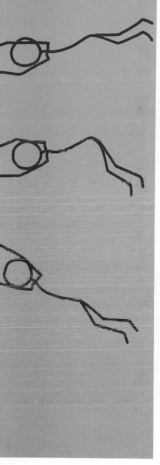

Players:
4–6 per group

Equipment:
trapeze or rings

Behavioral goal: To swing on the bar, then drop off safely.

Child grasps the bar or rings with both hands and starts momentum by taking a few running steps or by a push from a helper. He pumps with the body by arching and extending the legs. He continues swinging, pulling slightly on the bar at the height of the forward swing to aid momentum.

When ready to drop off, he keeps his body extended and at the height of the backswing he pulls on the bar, releases his grip and drops off to a stand, giving with the knees and ankles to minimize the jar of landing.

It is important for the child to have adult supervision while learning this skill, as he may need help in starting the momentum and in dropping from the bar or rings.

EVALUATIVE CHECK LIST

1. Is each child able to swing and drop successfully?
   a. Does he pump the body to gain momentum?
   b. At height of backswing, does he pull on the bar and drop to ground?

2. Does each child understand how to minimize the jar of landing?
   a. Can he "give" on landing by bending the knees and ankles?
   b. Does he spread feet to widen base of support?

3. Does the child understand how to regain balance when landing?
   a. Does he lower the center of gravity by bending knees?
   b. Does he widen the base of support by spreading feet apart?
   c. Does he carry weight forward, rocking forward to hands if necessary?

NOTES

174

Roll

Players:
4–6 per group

Equipment:
mats

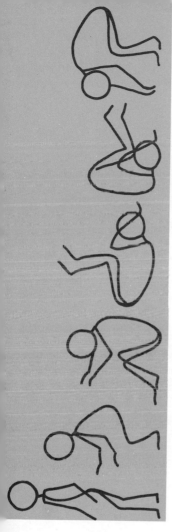

Behavioral goal: To do a back somersault by rolling backward with the body curled.

Child sits at edge of mat, knees bent, feet on the floor. He places his hands at his shoulders, palms up, thumbs toward neck. He pushes with his feet, tucks his head, and rocks backward, bringing knees close to chest. As his hips rock over his shoulders, he pushes against the mat with his hands, drops his toes on the mat in back of his head, taking his weight on them and finishing in a squat position.

EVALUATIVE CHECK LIST

1. Can each child perform the stunt successfully?
   a. Does he keep head tucked, carrying weight on hands as he rolls backward?
   b. Does he finish in squat position with weight on feet?

2. Does each child understand that to roll successfully he must lose balance?
   a. Does he push body off balance with feet?
   b. Does he keep body curled as he rolls?

   c. Does he use momentum to keep rolling to squat position?

3. Does each child have the courage to attempt the stunt?

4. Do children cooperate with each other?
   a. Do they avoid interfering with performer in any way?
   b. Do they give helpful suggestions if needed?

NOTES

Stand

Players:
4–6 per group

Equipment:
mats

Behavioral goal: To balance the body in a headstand position.

Child takes tripod position on the mat by placing his head about 10–12 inches in advance of his hands. The head and hands form a triangle base with the weight of the body over the center of the triangle. Child then slowly raises his legs until they are straight and above his head, arching his back to keep his center of gravity over the base of support. To return to starting position, child bends legs and drops them to the floor, or he may tuck his head, curl, and do a forward roll.

This stunt should be performed under adult supervision while the child is learning it, as he may need help in raising his legs, arching his back, and returning to starting position.

EVALUATIVE CHECK LIST

1. Does each child understand the importance of keeping his line of gravity over the base of support to maintain balance in this inverted position?

2. Does each child have the courage to attempt the stunt?

3. Does each child understand the importance of the "tripod" position in establishing a wide base to aid in balance?

4. Do children cooperate with each other while waiting for their turns?

   a. Do they avoid interfering with performance of others?

   b. Do they give helpful suggestions if needed?

NOTES

Door, Back Door

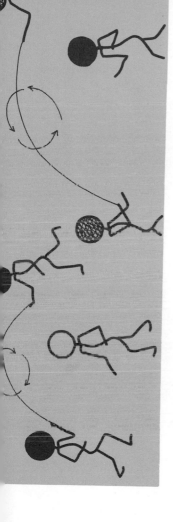

Players:
6–8 per group

Equipment:
one 18–20 foot rope per group

Behavioral goal: To run into a turning rope, jump, and run out.

Two children turn a long rope for other children to run into and jump. When the rope swings toward the jumper from above, it is called "front door" and when it swings toward him from below it is called "back door." Jumper runs in the front door immediately after the rope touches the ground, and in the back door immediately after it passes his body.

Children perform the following stunts:

1. *Run in the front door, jump once, run out.*

2. *Run in the front door, jump to the jingle, then run out:*

   Teddy Bear, Teddy Bear, turn around (turn while jumping,

   Teddy Bear, Teddy Bear, touch the ground (touch ground)

   Teddy Bear, Teddy Bear, show your shoe (raise foot in air)

   Teddy Bear, Teddy Bear, run on through (run out other side).

3. *Run in back door, jump once, run out.*

4. *Run in back door, jump to jingle, then run out:*

   I asked my mother for fifty cents
   To watch the monkey jump the fence,
   He jumped so high he reached the sky
   And didn't come down 'til the Fourth of July.

EVALUATIVE CHECK LIST

1. Is each child able to run into the rope, both front door and back door, jump several times, and run out?

2. Do rope turners accept their responsibilities in helping the jumper to succeed?

   a. Do they turn rope rhythmically?

   b. Are they certain that the rope touches the ground each time?

   c. When jumpers are having difficulty learning how to jump, do turners try to help them by swinging slower or faster as needed?

3. Does each child "give" with knees and ankles, landing lightly on feet?

NOTES

Balance Beam

Players:
4–6 per group

Equipment:
balance beam

Behavioral goal: To perform various stunts on the balance beam.

Children perform the following stunts on the beam:

1. Walk forward several steps ending in stride position, pivot without lifting feet from beam, and return.

2. Jump on the beam.

3. Hop on one foot.

4. Stand on one leg, swinging other leg forward and backward.

5. Sit, facing length of beam.

6. Sit, knees bent, then knees straight.

7. Do swan dive, standing on one leg and bending trunk forward with the other leg straight in air in back of body.

8. Do duck walk, squatting and taking three or four steps.

9. Gallop several steps.

10. Imitate a measuring worm, with weight on all fours, first walking forward with the hands while keeping feet stationary, then walking feet up to meet hands.

11. Make up their own stunts.

EVALUATIVE CHECK LIST

1. Does each child know how to maintain balance on the beam?

   a. Does he increase frictional resistance with clean shoes and clean beam?

   b. Does he center the line of gravity of the body over the feet?

   c. Does he lower the center of gravity by bending the knees?

   d. Does he widen the base of support by spreading the feet?

2. Does each child know how to regain equilibrium quickly after a temporary loss of balance?

   a. Does he spread the feet and bend the knees quickly?

   b. Does he extend arms to side, dipping one or the other to bring the center of gravity back over the feet?

3. Does each child have the courage to try each stunt?

4. Do children help each other when necessary?

NOTES

Click

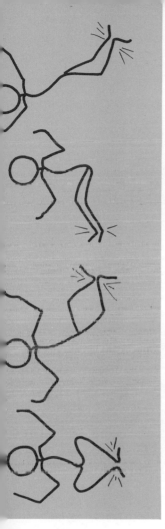

Players:
any number

Equipment:
none

Behavioral goal: To jump into the air and click the heels together before landing.

Child jumps from both feet into the air and clicks his heels together once before landing.

Variations:

1. Jump and click heels twice before landing.

2. Cross one foot in front of other, then spring upward from forward foot, lifting other foot sideward and clicking heels before landing on take-off foot.

3. Extend one foot forward, jumping from other foot and clicking heels, landing on take-off foot.

4. Extend one foot to the rear, leap from other foot and click heels in this position, landing on take-off foot.

EVALUATIVE CHECK LIST

1. Does each child know how to obtain the height necessary to perform the heel clicks before landing?

   a. Does he bend knees, flex ankles and push against the floor forcibly on the take-off?

   b. Does he swing arms forcibly upward for greater height?

2. Does each child know how to land without losing balance?

   a. Does he bend knees on landing to lower the center of gravity?

   b. Does he keep the line of gravity over the base of support?

   c. When landing on both feet, does he spread feet apart for wider base?

   d. When landing on one foot, does he extend arms to sides to help with equilibrium?

3. Does each child know how to absorb the shock of impact on landing?

   a. Does he land on balls of feet?

   b. Does he "give" on landing by bending knees and flexing ankles?

NOTES

from
an
Object

Players:
4–6 per group

Equipment:
box, horse, low ramp, or table

Behavioral goal: To jump from an object, landing in different ways.

Child sits or stands on a box, horse, low ramp, low bar, table, or other low object that will safely support his weight. He jumps off, landing on a mat, sand pit, sod, or some other appropriate surface. Challenges may include:

1. *Jump off, landing softly.*
2. *Jump off, walking in the air.*
3. *Jump off, bringing knees to chest, then straightening legs before landing.*
4. *Jump off, making a turn in the air.*
5. *Jump off, turning a forward roll after landing.*
6. *Jump off with a partner.*
7. *Try other ways of jumping off.*

EVALUATIVE CHECK LIST

1. Does each child know how to diminish the force of landing gradually to avoid injury?
   - a. Does he land on balls of feet, flexing ankles, knees, and hips?
   - b. Does he land on a soft surface?

2. Does each child know how to land without losing balance?

a. Does he keep center of gravity over the base of support (the feet)?
b. Does he spread the feet to give a larger base of support?

3. Is each child able to cooperate with a partner in jumping together from the object?

NOTES

Astronaut

Players:
4–6 per group

Equipment:
bar

Behavioral goal: To "walk" in space while suspended from a bar.

Child grasps bar with hands and hangs with arms and legs fully extended, feet completely off ground. From this position the child raises first one knee, then the other, continuing to walk without stopping. He receives one score for each step. Knee should be raised until thigh is parallel with floor.

The hanging position may help the child obtain a kinesthetic feeling for good body alignment from head to toes, if it is brought to his attention. Then when he stands again he tries to achieve the same body alignment as when he was hanging.

EVALUATIVE CHECK LIST

1. Is each child able to hang from the bar long enough to raise and lower his legs several times?

2. Does each child understand how suspending the body from the bar in this position improves arm strength? Does he understand that:

a. Arm muscles must work to hold the body in this position?

b. Increasingly longer periods of suspension will help to increase arm strength?

3. Does each child try to improve his score from day to day?

NOTES

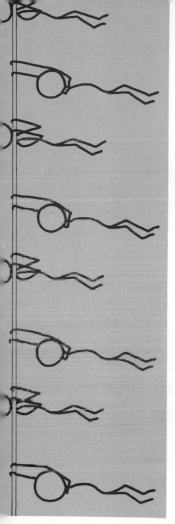

Players:
4–6 per group

Equipment:
bar

Behavioral goal: To chin oneself as many times as possible

Child jumps and grasps a bar that is slightly higher than his standing reach. He may grip the bar with a front or reverse grip. He then pulls himself toward his hands in an attempt to place his chin over the bar. The body is lowered back to the hanging position. The child repeats the pulling up and lowering movements until he can do no more.

Chinning with support: Chins may be difficult for some children and modified chins with the feet on the ground can be used until he develops the necessary strength for regular chinning. In the modified chin, the child grasps a low bar, palms toward himself. He extends his legs in front with knees bent at right angles, weight supported by feet and arms. He bends his elbows until his chin is level with the bar, then extends his arms to the original position. He continues for as long as possible.

EVALUATIVE CHECK LIST

1. Does each child understand how chinning will increase his arm and shoulder girdle strength?

a. Can he use these muscles in raising and lowering the body?

b. Does he understand that as the number of chins increases, strength increases?

2. If he is unable to chin himself, does each child know how to develop the arm strength needed?

a. Does he chin with support until he is able to do several with ease?

b. Does he chin with support from high bar by starting in position with elbows bent, then lowering the body (stand on a box to reach this position)?

c. When able to lower the body easily from the bent elbow position, does he practice raising and lowering the body without support?

3. Does each child try to improve his own score rather than competing with others?

NOTES

Ladder

Players:
4-6 per group

Equipment:
horizontal ladder

Behavioral goal: To "walk" with the hands on the horizontal ladder.

Child climbs steps and grasps first rung of the ladder. From a hanging position he reaches with one hand for the next rung and continues "walking" across ladder, alternating hands, from rung to rung.

Other stunts to be performed on the ladder:

1. Walk across the ladder with the hands, skipping every other rung.

2. Travel sideways, grasping one side of the ladder with both hands.

3. Travel forward, grasping both sides of the ladder, one hand on each side.

4. Make a half turn with the body as you swing from rung to rung.

5. Make up your own stunts on the ladder.

Slunts and Tests: grades 3, 4   191

EVALUATIVE CHECK LIST

1. Does each child have the courage to try the stunt?

2. Does each child have the arm strength to move from rung to rung on the ladder?

3. Does each child know how to develop the strength to perform the stunt, if he is unable to do so correctly?

   a. Does he practice other activities to improve arm strength, such as Flying Trapeze, Walking Astronaut, and chinning with and without support?

   b. Does he practice hanging from the ladder for longer periods each day?

   c. Does he practice "walking" just one or two rungs at a time, if he cannot walk across the entire ladder?

NOTES

Rolls
from a
Run

Players:
4–6 per group

Equipment:
mats

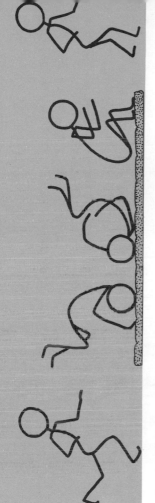

Behavioral goal: To run to the mat and perform several forward rolls.

Child takes a short run forward toward the mat, springs from both feet, landing on hands on mat, immediately bending elbows and tucking head under and rolling over. At finish of roll he keeps body curled, rocks weight over feet, and immediately rolls forward again. He continues rolls for the length of the mat, leaping to his feet after the last roll.

EVALUATIVE CHECK LIST

1. Can each child perform the stunt successfully?
   a. Does he take a short run (a few steps only) and roll on the mat without stopping?
   b. Does he avoid touching his head while rolling?
   c. At the finish of one roll, does he immediately rock forward into another roll?
   d. Does he leap to his feet after last roll?

2. Does each child understand that to roll successfully he must lose balance and rotate his body around its points of contact with the mat?
   a. Does he keep his body curled in a ball?
   b. Does he continue rolling motion by pushing off with feet each time they touch mat?
   c. Does he use momentum to continue rolling?

3. Does each child have the courage to attempt the stunt?

4. Do children cooperate with each other?
   a. Do they await turns quietly?
   b. Do they avoid interference with performer?
   c. Do they help each other when needed?

NOTES

Ropes

Players:
10–12 per group

Equipment:
two 18–20 foot ropes per group

Behavioral goal: To run into two crossed ropes, jump, and run out.

Children review jumping front door and back door, using a single long rope. Then two of the long ropes are crossed at right angles with each other, with a rope turner at the end of each rope (four turners). Rope turners synchronize ropes so that both are turning toward the jumper from above (front door) and are touching the ground simultaneously. All four turners must work together to synchronize the turning. Child runs into front door to the center where the ropes cross and jumps several times, then runs out.

Variations:

1. Run in the front door, jump to the jingle, then run out:

   One, two buckle my shoe;
   Three, four, shut the door;
   Five, six, pick up sticks;
   Seven, eight, lay them straight;
   Nine, ten, run out again.

2. Run in the back door (ropes both swinging toward jumper from below) and jump to the jingle, then run out.

3. Run in the back door carrying a short jumping rope and jump the short rope in the center of the crossed ropes.

4. One child jumps the short rope in center of crossed ropes and a partner runs in and jumps with him.

5. Make up your own rope tricks.

EVALUATIVE CHECK LIST

1. Is each child able to run into the crossed ropes, both front and back door, jump several times, and run out?

2. Do the four rope turners synchronize their ropes so they touch the ground simultaneously?

3. Does each jumper land lightly on the balls of his feet and push off rhythmically?

4. Do children attempt many of the stunts, practicing them until they are successful?

NOTES

Balance Beam

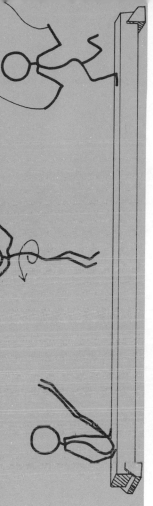

Players:
4–6 per group

Equipment:
balance beam

Behavioral goal: To perform many stunts on the balance beam.

Beam should be 8–10 inches from the floor, with mats on either side of it for safety. Children review stunts performed on beam in previous grades, then try to perform new stunts. Challenges may include:

1. Hop on one foot, forward and backward.
2. Turn on beam in squat position by crouching with one foot ahead of the other, then making a half pivot turn without rising.
3. V-sit on the beam by sitting, then lifting both legs until the body and legs form a V.
4. Perform half-top on beam, jumping into air and turning halfway around.
5. Jump rope on the beam.
6. Make up your own stunts, performed singly or with a partner.

EVALUATIVE CHECK LIST

1. Does each child understand how to apply the following principles of stability?

   a. Stability is greater when the center of gravity is lowered, the base of support is enlarged, and the line of gravity is more nearly over the base (knees bent, feet apart, body aligned over feet).

   b. The greater the mass of the body, the greater the stability (heavy people are more stable than light people).

   c. The greater the frictional resistance between the supporting surface and the body, the greater the stability (for example, clean tennis shoes on a clean beam).

   d. When moving under difficult conditions, stability is improved when eyes are fixed on a stationary spot at or above eye level.

2. Does each child have the courage to attempt the more difficult stunts?

3. Do children follow safety rules?

   a. Are there mats on either side of low beam?

   b. Do children avoid distracting performers?

   c. Do they use "spotters" to assist performers on more difficult stunts, in which falling may cause injury?

   d. Is only one performer (or performers involved in a group stunt) on the beam at one time?

NOTES

Arch

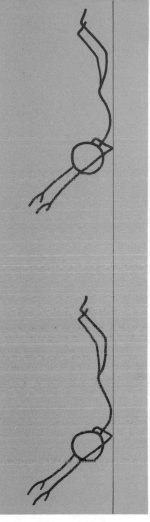

Players:
any number

Equipment:
none

Behavioral goal: To arch back and raise chest and thighs from floor for a count of 3.

Child lies face down, hands over head. He raises his head and toes from the floor, attempting to clear his chest and thighs from the floor. He holds the position for a count of three, then returns to the original position. Repeat several times.

EVALUATIVE CHECK LIST

1. Does each child understand that this exercise will strengthen his back extensors?

2. Is each child able to perform the stunt correctly at least one time?

   a. Can he clear chest and thighs from floor?
   b. Can he hold for a count of three?

3. Does each child try to hold for a longer count, or repeat the count three exercise a greater number of times during succeeding days?

4. Does each child understand what strength is and how it is developed? Does he understand:

   a. The ability of muscles to work to overcome resistance?

   b. That one develops strength by overloading the muscle:

   (1) by increasing the load to be moved;
   (2) by increasing the number of repetitions;
   (3) by increasing the rate?

NOTES

Roll
over a
Mat

Players:
4–6 per group

Equipment:
mats

Behavioral goal: To dive over an obstacle and do a forward roll.

A rolled-up mat is placed at the edge of another mat. The child takes several running steps toward the mat, and when about a foot from it he jumps forward and upward, landing with his hands on the other side of the rolled-up mat. He bends elbows, tucks head, and rolls over the obstacle, returning to his feet.

Variations: When the child can perform the above easily, he may try other dives. Challenges may include:

1. *Dive over one person who is lying flat on the edge of the mat.*

2. *Dive over one person who is crouched on hands and knees.*

3. *Dive over one person who is raised high on hands and knees.*

4. *Dive over two people who are crouched side by side.*

5. *Make up your own dives.*

Stunts and Tests: grades 5, 6   201

EVALUATIVE CHECK LIST

1. Can each child perform the stunt successfully?
   a. Can he take a short run, dive, and roll on the mat without stopping?
   b. Can he avoid touching the obstacle?
   c. Can he avoid touching his head while rolling?
   d. Can he leap to his feet after rolling once?

2. Does each child have the courage to attempt the stunt?

3. Do children cooperate with each other?
   a. Do they await turns without interfering with performers?
   b. Do they give helpful suggestions to each other and "spot" for each other when necessary?

NOTES

the
Cat

Players:
4–6 per group

Equipment:
low bar

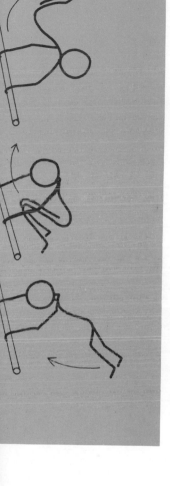

Behavioral goal: To "skin the cat" on the low bar.

Child grasps bar, palms of hands toward him. He lifts knees up between arms, and bringing them to his chest, he lowers his head and simultaneously swings legs through arms, turning over and touching the ground with his toes, releasing bar, and standing.

Variation: After turning over, retain grasp on bar, touch toes to ground and immediately turn body back to original position, bringing legs back through arms and ending in standing position facing bar.

EVALUATIVE CHECK LIST

1. Does each child have the courage to attempt the stunt?

2. Does each child have the strength to support his weight while turning over on the bar?

3. Does child know how to help himself develop sufficient arm strength to perform the stunt?

   a. Does he practice Walking Astronaut, chinning, walking on horizontal ladder?

   b. Does he practice lifting knees between arms and holding this position with assistance (if needed) over increasingly longer periods of time?

4. Do children help each other?

   a. Do they avoid interfering with the performer?

   b. Do they give assistance by "spotting" for a performer when necessary?

NOTES

204

Broad Jump

Players:
4–6 per group

Equipment:
mat or jumping pit

Behavioral goal: To jump forward as far as possible.

Child stands at edge of mat or jumping pit, feet in back of take-off line. He swings his arms, bends his knees, and jumps forward as far as possible. His score is the number of inches measured from the take-off line to the heel, or nearest point touched by his body in landing. Child is allowed three trials, and the best score of the three is recorded.

EVALUATIVE CHECK LIST

1. Does each child know how to get the greatest distance from his jump?

a. Does he bend knees, hips, and ankles and push off from the floor as long as possible (because the longer the force is applied, the greater the height and distance)?

b. Does he push primarily backward with feet to move the body forward?

c. Does he swing arms forcibly forward and upward as the body leaves the floor (because the momentum of any part of a supported body can be transferred to the body as a whole)?

2. Does each child know how to absorb the shock of impact on landing?

a. Does he land on balls of feet, immediately bending knees, ankles, and hips and giving with the movement?

b. Does he land on a soft surface?

c. Does he land with feet apart, weight carried forward, tipping forward to the hands if necessary with arms giving at wrists, elbows, and shoulders?

3. Does each child practice to improve his jumping distance?

NOTES

the Shot

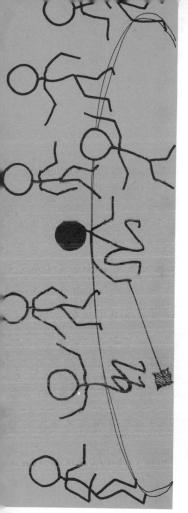

Players:
8–10 per group

Equipment:
soft tennis shoe or beanbag tied to one
12–15-foot rope per group

Behavioral goal: To jump into the air and clear the shot.

Each group of children forms a circle facing the center. One child holds the "shot" in the center of the circle. The shot is a soft tennis shoe or beanbag tied to the end of a 12–15-foot rope.

Child in the center kneels and starts swinging the shot around the circle. As it reaches a circle player he must jump into the air to clear it. Any player tagged by the shot must drop out of the game. Winner is the last child to remain in the circle.

The shot must be swung so that it never is more than 5 or 6 inches off the floor. Children should practice swinging the shot before playing the game.

EVALUATIVE CHECK LIST

1. Can each child clear the shot successfully when it reaches him?

   a. Does he bend knees and push off vertically?

   b. Does he swing arms forcibly upward to gain height?

2. Does each child know how to maintain balance and lessen the shock of impact when landing?

   a. Does he keep feet in stride position?

   b. Does he keep knees and ankles flexed, landing on "rubber" legs?

3. Can each child swing the shot successfully when it is his turn?

   a. Does he change rope from hand to hand to keep it going in a wide arc?

   b. Does he swing it no more than 5 or 6 inches from the floor?

   c. Does he hold balance in squat position while swinging?

NOTES

Beater

Players:
6–8 per group

Equipment:
two 15–20 foot ropes per group

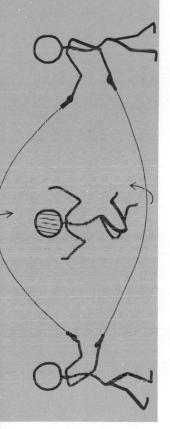

Behavioral goal: To jump two ropes that are turning toward each other alternately.

Two children, holding the end of a rope in each hand, turn two long ropes alternately toward each other. A child runs in at the center and jumps the ropes. He must jump rapidly in order to jump over both ropes alternately as they come under his feet in sequence.

When the child is adept at this, he may run into the "egg beater" (alternating ropes) carrying a short rope and jump his short rope as he jumps the long ropes.

EVALUATIVE CHECK LIST

1. Is each child able to run into egg beater, jump several times, and run out?

2. Do the two rope turners accept their responsibility for helping the jumper if he needs it?

   a. Do they turn the ropes alternately in rhythm, using the jumper's rhythm if necessary?

   b. Do they make certain that the ropes touch the ground each time?

3. Does each jumper land lightly and push off rhythmically?

NOTES

THROWING AND CATCHING

Throwing an object is applying muscular force to develop momentum, which can be transferred to an external object. For example, when a ball is thrown it attains the speed of the hand and when released will continue in the direction of the application of force, tangent to the arc where released until gravity or other external forces alter its path. The longer the sequential development of force can be applied to the ball before its release, the farther and faster it will travel.

force is preceded by a backswing, which places future contributing muscles on a stretch. The forward momentum in the desired direction of the throw is begun as a step is taken with the foot away from the throwing arm. This step causes the center of gravity to begin to move in the direction of the throw. Pushing off the back foot and rotation of the trunk then occur, continuing up to the shoulder. The elbow is then pulled forward, preceding the ball, and the final forces are added by a strong extension of the elbow and flexion of the wrist and fingers just prior to the release. The faster the hand is moving at this point the faster the ball will travel.

It is sometimes helpful to think of the arm as a "whip" pulling on the ball. This comparison will insure that the elbow is positioned in front of the ball so that the tendency to push on the ball is eliminated. The underhand throw differs from the overhand throw only in that the ball is held closer to the body with a straight arm, which swings like a pendulum.

Skill in catching a moving object is the ability to coordinate the act of receiving impetus from the moving object. The object must be gradually slowed until it can be grasped. As the object approaches the catcher, he reaches toward it, keeping the elbows and knees slightly bent. The knees will bend more if a heavier or larger object is to be caught. The body must be in a position to permit body levers to move with the object as force is being applied to slow it down. The object should not be allowed to strike the hands when the arms are extended and elbows locked. A ball will strike the heels of the hands and almost invariably rebound away from the grasp.

The catcher watches the object approach his hands and will usually begin moving his hands in the direction of the object's movement just as contact is made. If the object is light, the force can be absorbed in the hands and arms. Heavier or larger objects will require the involvement of larger body segments, such as shoulders, back and legs. Beginners should be encouraged to catch with both hands, because doing so increases the grasping action and the area for catching.

Kindergarten children enjoy manipulating objects to find out how they "feel" and what they can do. Balls of different sizes and weights, beanbags, and rings should be available for children to handle, bounce, toss, roll, or use in any ways they devise. Four and five year olds may prefer to select and manipulate objects individually rather than joining in group activities using objects. The simplest group activities for children of this age are handling equipment, rolling or pushing balls, and bouncing balls.

Older children are capable of performing many different types of overhand and underhand throws using various sizes and types of balls. Ten, eleven and twelve year olds are interested in improving their throwing-catching skills to aid successful performance in many of the culturally acceptable sports such as football, basketball, softball. These status activities are particularly important to boys of this age group, and their need to excel in one or more of these sports is a motivating factor toward improving skills and working on new skills.

and Farmer Brown

Players:
any number

Equipment:
large and small balls, box, beanbag, block

Behavioral goal: To pass objects around the circle without dropping them.

Children and teacher sit in a circle on the floor. Teacher tells story as she passes objects around the circle. Objects should be handed from child to child and returned to the teacher after they have been passed around the circle.

"Mother Rabbit started to look for Peter, who had been gone from home for some time." (Teacher takes a large ball and passes it slowly to a child next to her and it continues slowly around the circle.)

"She couldn't find him so she decided to wait for him

at home." (Teacher places ball back in box when it returns to her.)

"Meanwhile, Peter was taking a walk in Farmer Brown's lettuce patch." (Teacher starts small ball slowly around circle.) "Farmer Brown saw him and took after him." (Pass large ball after small ball, moving both balls as rapidly as possible around the circle.)

If Farmer Brown overtakes Peter before he gets home, Peter is caught. He may escape and get home, Mother

Rabbit may find him, or the story may end in any way the teacher and children decide. Other characters may be added to the story, such as Flopsy Rabbit (the beanbag), the Fox (the block), and so on.

EVALUATIVE CHECK LIST

1. Can each child receive and pass the object without dropping it?

2. Can each child maintain the emotional control needed to pass the objects rapidly without dropping them?

3. Are children creative in helping the teacher decide on other characters for the story?

4. Do children avoid criticizing negatively if errors are made by classmates?

NOTES

Ball

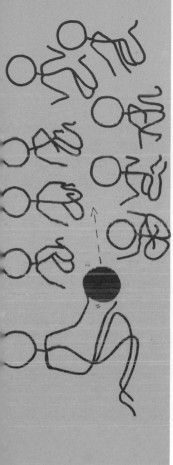

Players:
8–10 per group

Equipment:
rubber utility ball for each group

Behavioral goal: To push or roll the ball away from oneself quickly.

Teacher and children sit in circle. Teacher places both hands on a rubber utility ball, which is sitting in front of her. She says, "I am warming the ball." Then she suddenly says, "The ball is hot!" and quickly pushes it away from her, using both hands. As it rolls across the circle to a child, he pushes it away with both hands. This continues until the ball rolls away or the teacher starts a new game.

Teacher may ask a child to warm the ball and start the game. Teacher and children may vary the game by pushing the ball with only one hand, or by standing in a circle and bouncing the ball.

EVALUATIVE CHECK LIST

1. Is each child able to control the ball when pushing it with both hands?

2. Do children try to push the ball in different directions to give each child a turn?

3. Are children able to "warm" the ball and play the game by themselves?

NOTES

Roll the Ball to . . .

Players:
8–10 per group

Equipment:
utility balls of different sizes

Behavioral goal: To roll the ball to another person, using one or two hands.

Teacher and children sit on floor in circle. Teacher has a rubber utility ball. He says, for example "I'll roll the ball to Mary," and rolls the ball to her. Child stops the ball with both hands, then rolls it with both hands to another child, saying first, "I'll roll the ball to. . . ."

Game continues until all have received the ball several times. Then teacher takes a different-sized ball and starts a new game, using only one hand to roll the ball. Children stop the ball with one hand, using the same hand to roll it to someone else. Teacher may ask a child to be leader of the group.

Game continues, using different-sized balls and one or two hands as designated by the leader. A variation may be standing and bouncing the balls.

EVALUATIVE CHECK LIST

1. Are children improving in ability to control different-sized balls with one or two hands?

2. Do children see that everyone has a turn by calling names of those who have not played?

3. Is each child able to take his turn at being leader of his group?

a. Can he decide on the ball to be used?

b. Can he decide whether to use one or two hands?

c. Can he start the game?

NOTES

and
Catch

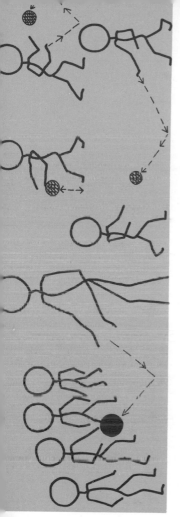

Players:
10–20

Equipment:
1 rubber ball per player

Behavioral goal: To bounce and catch a rubber playground ball.

Each child has a rubber ball. He bounces it and catches it, using both hands, repeating the sequence several times. Then he tries to bounce his ball to a partner and catch the partner's return bounce.

Children bounce a ball against a wall and catch it as it bounces back. Teacher places several children in a line and bounces to each in turn.

Children experiment with other ways of bouncing and catching, for example:

1. Can you bounce the ball hard so it rebounds over your head, and catch it on the fly?
2. Can you bounce the ball hard and catch it on the second bounce?
3. Can you bounce the ball and turn around before you catch it?
4. Can you toss the ball into the air and catch it on the first bounce?
5. How many times can you bounce the ball against the wall and catch it when it bounces back?

Throwing and Catching: Kindergarten   219

6. Can you bounce the ball against the wall and catch it before it bounces back (on the fly)?

EVALUATIVE CHECK LIST

1. Can each child control the rebound by bouncing hard or easy? Straight down or at an angle?

2. Can each child judge the rebound and catch the ball on the fly?

3. Are children able to bounce and catch balls with partners?

a. Can they estimate the force needed in relation to the distance to be covered?

b. Can they be in position to catch the ball?

4. Are children innovative in finding many new ways to bounce the ball?

NOTES

Shot

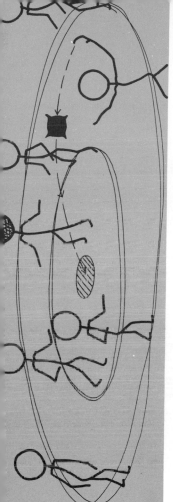

Players:
6–8 per group

Equipment:
1 beanbag per group

Behavioral goal: To throw the beanbag and hit the "moon."

Each child stands on the inner circle and, in turn tries to "shoot the moon" with the beanbag. "Moon" is a small circle inside two larger circles (see illustration). If child is successful he moves to the outer circle and shoots from there when his turn comes again.

When a child makes a successful throw, he moves to or remains on the outer circle. When he is unsuccessful he remains on or returns to the inner circle. Each suc-cessful throw from the inner circle counts 1 point, and from the outer circle, 2 points.

Center player is retriever and throws beanbag to each player in turn, or each player may retrieve his own beanbag and pass to the next player. After the beanbag has gone around the circle once, the retriever (if one is used) chooses a player from the outer circle to be the new retriever and exchanges places with him.

EVALUATIVE CHECK LIST

1. Does each child understand the game rules and move to the appropriate circle without coaching?

2. Do children use one-hand underhand toss in throwing at the target?

3. Is each child learning to use a relaxed, swinging movement of the arm, stepping forward on the opposite foot, toward the target?

4. Does each child who is retrieving make accurate passes to the circle players?

NOTES

Choice

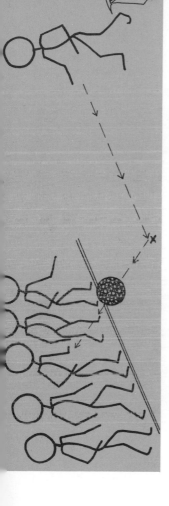

Players:
6–8 per group

Equipment:
different-sized balls, beanbags

Behavioral goal: To throw and catch different-sized balls.

Children stand on line facing child who is "teacher." "Teacher" chooses any ball he wishes to use and throws or bounces it to each child in turn. When each child has received the ball, "teacher" goes to end of line and child who is at head of line becomes the new "teacher," choosing the ball to be used. Game continues until each child has been "teacher."

EVALUATIVE CHECK LIST

1. Are children experimenting with different ways of *giving* impetus to different size objects?

   a. Do they throw underhand or overhand, using one hand, when throwing beanbag?

   b. Do they throw balls underhand, overhand, with one hand, with two hands, or using bounce, depending upon size of ball?

2. Are children learning how to *receive* impetus from different sized objects?

   a. Do they catch with palms of hands toward object?

   b. Do they keep elbows and knees "easy" when catching?

   c. Do they give with the catch?

3. Do children help each other to succeed?

   a. Do they throw balls that are easy to catch (not hard throws at close range)?

   b. Do they consider abilities of receiver and throw accordingly?

NOTES

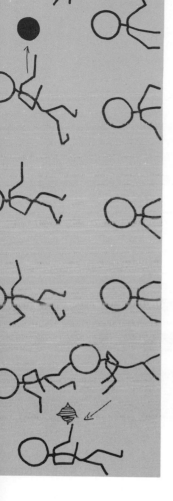

and
Squirrel

Players:
8–10 per group

Equipment:
8-inch ball, beanbag per group

Behavioral goal: To toss objects rapidly around the circle.

Children stand in a circle. A ball, the "fox," is held by a child in the circle opposite a child who is holding the "squirrel," a beanbag. On signal "Go!" both objects are started around the circle in the same direction, the fox trying to overtake the "squirrel." The "fox" may change direction around the circle at any time. The "squirrel" must then change direction to avoid being caught.

EVALUATIVE CHECK LIST

1. Is each child able to maintain control during the excitement of the game, and make good throws and catches?

2. Are children able to determine strategic times for changing the direction of the "fox"?

3. Is the child with the "squirrel" able to reach immediately to the change in direction?

4. Do children experiment with other objects as "fox" and "squirrel," such as:
   a. Different sizes and weights of balls?
   b. Blocks of wood?
   c. Balloon, rings, unbreakable toys, and so on?

NOTES

Ball

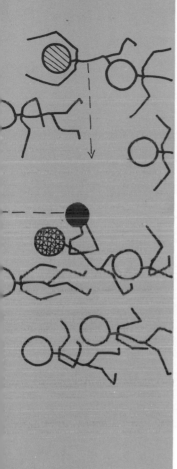

Players:
8–10 per group

Equipment:
8-inch ball per group

Behavioral goal: To toss a ball straight into the air; to catch a ball on the bounce or fly.

Children stand around outside of circle with one child in the center holding an 8-inch utility ball. Child in center calls name of a circle player, simultaneously tossing the ball straight into the air.

Player whose name is called must catch ball on the fly before it touches the ground. If he is successful, he becomes IT and goes to the center to call a name. If the player who is called misses the ball, he remains where he is and the original IT gets to toss again.

A legal toss is one that goes at least 6 feet over the head of the tosser and would land on the inside of the circle. If the toss is not legal, child whose name was called gets to be IT whether or not he catches the ball.

If children are not skillful enough to catch the ball on the fly, one bounce may be permitted.

EVALUATIVE CHECK LIST

1. Can each child toss the ball straight into the air?
   a. Can he bend knees, then straighten body upward?
   b. Can he lift ball straight up and follow through with hands and arms?

2. Can each child judge accurately where the ball will land and put himself in position to catch it?

3. Can child who is IT successfully perform the dual role of calling a child's name at the same time as he tosses the ball into the air?

4. Do children see that all players have a turn at being called?

NOTES

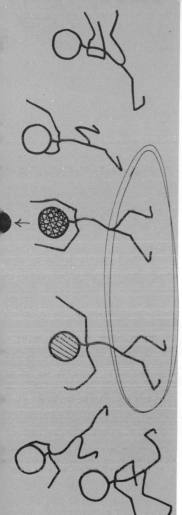

Behavioral goal: To catch a fly ball; to hit a stationary target with the ball.

Players:
8–10 per group

Equipment:
8-inch rubber ball per group

Children stand inside a circle, with one child in the center, holding an 8-inch rubber ball. Child with the ball tosses it high into the air, calling another child's name. The child called runs to catch the ball while all other children scatter into the playing field.

When the child catches the ball he calls, "Stop!" All other children must stop and freeze in their position, and may not move thereafter. Child with ball takes aim and tries to hit one of the others with the ball. If he hits a player fairly, below the waist, he takes the ball back to the center of the circle; other players return to the circle, and he calls a name and tosses the ball. If the thrower misses the player at whom he aimed, that person gets to toss the ball from center and call a name.

If a player is hit fairly he has a "spud" on him. After a player gets three spuds, he must pay a forfeit. The forfeit is predetermined at the time the game starts. The child may have to sing a song, run around the field, do a dance, stay out of the game until someone else gets three spuds, and so on.

Variation: if needed, a rule may be added permitting the thrower one or two giant steps toward the target before throwing.

EVALUATIVE CHECK LIST

1. Is IT able to coordinate calling the name and tossing the ball simultaneously?

2. Does each child know how to stop quickly?
   a. Does he lower the center of gravity by bending the knees?
   b. Does he widen the base of support in a stride position?
   c. Does he keep the line of gravity over the base to maintain balance?

3. Does each child know how to throw successfully at a stationary target?
   a. Does he take careful aim and keep eyes on target?
   b. Does he move center of body toward the target by stepping forward on the foot opposite the throwing arm?

4. Do children call names of those in the group who have not been IT, thus giving each child an opportunity to throw at the target?

NOTES

Dodge
Ball

Players:
8–10 per group

Equipment:
8-inch rubber ball per group

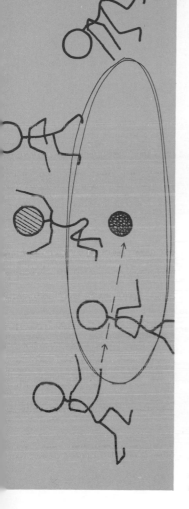

Behavioral goal: To hit a moving target with a ball; to dodge and avoid being hit by the ball.

Children stand outside a circle with one child on the inside. Outside players try to hit child in the center of the circle, using an 8-inch rubber ball. A fair hit is one that lands below the waist and is thrown by a player with both feet outside the circle.

When the center player is hit fairly he exchanges places with the thrower who hit him and the game continues.

EVALUATIVE CHECK LIST

1. Is each child improving in his ability to hit a moving target?

2. Is each child alert and able to catch balls thrown in his direction?

3. Is center child improving in ability to dodge and change direction rapidly to avoid being hit?

4. Are children able to identify a "fair hit" as one in which:

   a. Thrower's feet are outside of circle?
   b. Ball hits center player below the waist?

5. Are children considerate of each other?

   a. Do they avoid hard throws at close range?
   b. Do they give all circle players opportunities to throw the ball?

NOTES

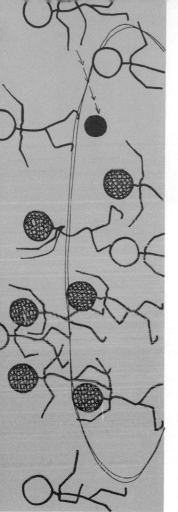

and
Dodgers

Players:
16–20 per group

Equipment:
8-inch rubber ball per group

Behavioral goal: To hit a moving target with a ball; to dodge and avoid being hit.

A circle is drawn on the floor. Half the children stand outside the circle as the "throwers" and half stand inside the circle as the "dodgers." Throwers stand with both feet outside the circle and try to hit the dodgers with an 8-inch rubber ball. The ball must land below the waist of the person who is hit.

When a dodger is hit, he joins the throwers and tries to hit other dodgers. Winner is the dodger who can stay in the circle the longest. Game is repeated, with players who were dodgers becoming throwers and throwers becoming dodgers. Game may end in a play-off between the two winners if so desired.

Variation: If a "dodger" can catch and hold a ball being thrown at him, he saves himself and remains in the circle.

EVALUATIVE CHECK LIST

1. Is each child learning how to hit a moving target?

2. Is each child learning how to dodge the thrown ball by stopping, starting, and changing direction quickly?

3. Do the children who are "dodgers" demonstrate consideration for each other?

   a. Do they avoid stepping on or running into others?

   b. Do they avoid pushing others into the ball to save themselves?

4. Do children who are "throwers" show consideration for others?

   a. Do they aim below the waist to avoid injuring players?

   b. Do they avoid hard throws at close range?

NOTES

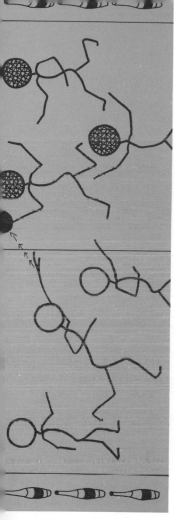

Players:
12–20 per group

Equipment:
8 Indian clubs and an 8-inch rubber ball per group

Behavioral goal: To knock down the opponents' clubs with the ball; to protect one's own clubs from the ball.

Group divides into two teams, one team in each court. Players may move freely on their own court.

One player holds a rubber ball; on the signal "Go!" he throws the ball at opponents' Indian clubs, trying to knock them down. Players continue throwing at opponents' clubs, at the same time protecting their own clubs, until one team knocks down all clubs of the other team. If the game is played for time, the team that knocks down the most clubs within the time limit wins.

Variation: As children's abilities improve, two or more balls may be introduced, thus making the game more difficult; rubber balls may be of different sizes, making it necessary for players to adjust rapidly to different sizes and weights.

Throwing and Catching: grades 3, 4   235

EVALUATIVE CHECK LIST

1. Is each child able to throw a fast, low ball aimed at the target?
   a. Does he take careful aim and keep eyes on target?
   b. Does he move center of body toward the target by stepping forward on the foot opposite the throwing arm?

2. Can each child successfully block or catch a hard-thrown ball?
   a. Can he block with hip or shoulder?
   b. Can he catch with palms of hands toward ball?
   c. Does he give with the block or catch?

3. Is each child alert and able to move quickly as the need arises?

4. Do children learn how to cooperate as a team?
   a. Do they decide on the best placement of players on the court?
   b. Do they pass to players who are in more strategic position for throwing?

NOTES

Ball

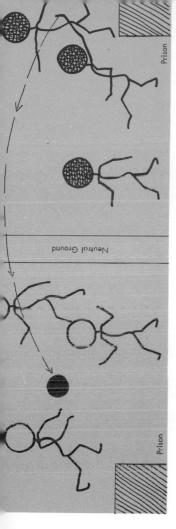

Prison

Neutral Ground

Prison

Players:
12–20 per group

Equipment:
any type of ball

Behavioral goal: To throw a ball, placing it out of reach of opponents; to catch a thrown ball.

Children divide into two teams with each team stationed in one court. Between courts is neutral ground. Each team has a "prison" on the side of its court. Ball is started by a player on one team, who calls the name of an opponent and throws the ball across the neutral ground into the opponents' court. Ball must be caught before it touches the ground or the player whose name was called must go to prison. Any player on the team may catch the ball. If it is caught successfully, the catcher calls an opponent's name and throws it into the opponents' court.

A team may free a prisoner by calling his name as the ball is thrown into the opponents' court. If the ball is *not* caught, the prisoner may return to his own team. If the ball lands in neutral ground it is dead. Team opposite the thrower recovers the ball. Game continues for 10 minutes. At end of the time period, the team with the most prisoners in prison *at that time* is the winner.

Note: Any type of ball may be used (football, basketball, softball, rubber playground ball, volleyball, and so on).

Throwing and Catching: grades 3, 4   237

EVALUATIVE CHECK LIST

1. Do all children have the strength and skill to throw the ball the necessary distance?

   a. Can they use both hands on the ball if necessary?

   b. Can they step toward the target on the foot opposite the throwing side?

2. Do children learn how to use strategy?

   a. Do they send the skillful opponents to prison?

   b. Do they try to recover their own skilled teammates from prison?

3. Are children able to accept results gracefully?

   a. Do they go to "prison" without complaint?

   b. Do they accept defeat without alibi?

4. Do skillful players try to help less skilled classmates?

   a. Do they give other players opportunities to throw and catch in the game situation?

   b. Do they practice with them whenever possible?

   c. Do they encourage rather than criticise or deride?

NOTES

Man

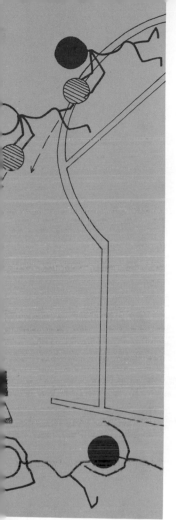

Players:
8–12 per group

Equipment:
basketball, goal

Behavioral goal: To shoot a basket before the opponent scores.

Players divide into two teams, 4–6 players per team. Number 1 player for each team is called "head man" and takes position in back of free throw line. Last man on each team stands under the basket, retrieves ball for his head man, and passes back to him.

On signal "Go!" both head men begin to shoot and continue shooting until one of them makes a goal, or until each one has shot three times. Player who first makes a goal scores 1 point for his team. If neither player scores after three trials, number 2 players become new head men and number 1 players become retrievers. Rotation continues after each goal, or after each three trials until all have been head men. Team with most points wins.

EVALUATIVE CHECK LIST

1. Does each child have the strength and skill to shoot the ball into the basket?

   a. Does he take careful aim, eyes on target, feet in forward stride position?

   b. Does he grip the ball at sides, with fingers spread?

   c. Does he bend knees, then straighten ankles, knees, hips, and elbows as he pushes ball forward and upward toward basket?

   d. Does he release ball and follow through with hands pointing toward basket and weight forward?

2. Does each child know how to analyze his own problems and improve his shooting?

   a. Can he improve arm strength if necessary?

   b. Does he extend body forcibly toward basket as ball is released?

3. Do players cooperate by retrieving ball quickly? Do they avoid distracting throwers?

NOTES

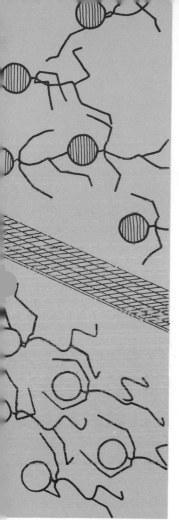

Players:
12–16 per group

Equipment:
volleyball, net

Behavioral goal: To throw a ball over the net; to catch a thrown ball before it hits the ground.

Players divide into two teams, each team on its own volleyball court. Each court is about 25 by 25 feet; top of net is about 5 feet from ground. Players arrange themselves to cover area on own court.

An 8-inch rubber playground ball is given to a player on one team, and on signal "Go!" a player throws the ball over the net into opponents' court. Opponents try to catch ball before it strikes the ground and throw it back over the net. If the ball hits the ground in either court at any time, 1 point is scored for the other team.

Ball is started again on the side where it hit the ground.

An out-of-bounds ball is brought in on the side where it went out and is put into play again. Players may not walk with the ball. They may pass to other teammates if they wish, but if the ball hits the ground on their court, 1 point is given to the opponents.

The penalty for walking with the ball is that the ball is awarded to the other team. The team with most points after a 10-minute playing period is the winner.

EVALUATIVE CHECK LIST

1. Is each child learning how to throw and catch a "hard" pass?

   a. Does he use one or two hands to throw ball, as needed?

   b. Does he step toward the net on foot opposite throwing side?

   c. Does he direct the ball toward the ground of opponents' court?

   d. Does he give with the ball when catching it?

2. Do children and teacher decide together on game rules, discarding old ones and adding new ones as needed?

3. Do children think through and know what to do in the game situation?

4. Does each team give all members opportunities to throw and catch the ball?

5. Do children cooperate as a team?

   a. Do they play own positions?

   b. Do they avoid interfering with other players?

NOTES

Basketball

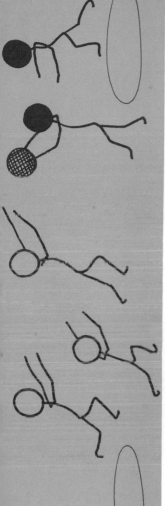

Players:
10–20 per group

Equipment:
1 basketball per group

Behavioral goal: To score a point for one's team by bouncing the ball in the opponents' target.

Children divide into two teams. Two circles, each 3½ feet in diameter, are drawn on the floor at either end of the basketball court. The game is started by one team member who receives the ball from the referee at his own end line. Players pass the ball to teammates in an effort to bounce it into their opponents' circle (target), while their opponents try to intercept the ball and bounce it into the opposite circle. Each time the ball is bounced in the opponents' target it scores 1 point for the team who hits the target.

After a score is made, the team opposite the scoring team receives the ball at its own end line and play continues.

The ball may be bounced or passed from player to player, but only one step is permitted when a player has possession of the ball. No dribbling is allowed. Fouls include:

1. *taking more than one step when in possession of the ball;*
2. *dribbling;*

3. *unnecessary roughness, such as pushing or kicking when intercepting a pass;*

4. *holding the ball for longer than 5 seconds.*

EVALUATIVE CHECK LIST

1. Are children able to work with teammates in keeping the ball away from the opponents as they work it down to the target?

   a. Do they keep the ball moving toward the target?

   b. Do they pass to players who are in position to hit the target?

2. Is each child improving his ability to pass and catch with accuracy?

Penalty for all fouls: Score if made, does not count and the ball is awarded to the opposite team at the point where the foul occurred.

3. Are children learning how to intercept passes skillfully without injury to other players?

4. Are children improving in ability to hit the target from increasingly greater distances?

NOTES

Behavioral goal: To hit other players with ball; to avoid being hit.

Two children are the Bombers and stand opposite each other outside of the circle. Other players are inside the circle. Bombers try to hit other players with the ball. A fair hit must land below the waist, and the ball must have been thrown from outside the circle.

When a player is hit fairly, he joins the Bombers on the outside of the circle and helps hit the remaining players. The two players who remain the longest in the circle become Bombers for the next game.

EVALUATIVE CHECK LIST

1. Are throwers able to use a variety of passes, as the situation demands?

    a. Do they avoid "hard" throws at close range?

    b. Do they work for accuracy rather than power?

2. Do players in circle anticipate direction of ball and move away from it accordingly?

    a. Do they avoid pushing other players?

    b. Do they move quickly to dodge or jump over the ball?

3. Is each child able to solve game problems quickly?

    a. Does he acknowledge a fair hit?

    b. Does he move quickly to a new position in the outer circle?

NOTES

Choice

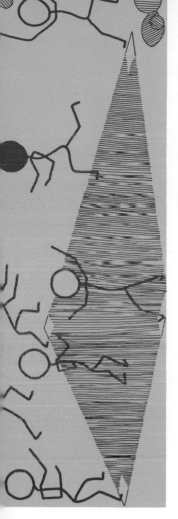

Players:
14–20 per group

Equipment:
different types and sizes of balls

Group divides into two teams, one at bat and the other in the field. Fielders play regular softball positions. A box of different types and sizes of balls (softball, football, basketball, utility balls) is placed behind home plate. The "batter" chooses any ball he wishes and throws it into the field, then runs to first base, second, third, and home without stopping on any base. If he gets home without being put out, he scores 1 point for his team.

Behavioral goal: To make a long throw into the field and run from first base to second, third, and home before the ball reaches the baseman.

Batter may not stop at any base but *must* continue toward home.

Batters are out if:

1. *fielder catches a fly ball;*
2. *fielder throws the ball to a baseman before the runner reaches the base (but the ball must have been thrown in order from first to second, third and home); each baseman*

must have one foot touching his base as he throws to the next baseman;

3. batter throws foul ball outside of playing area;

4. base runner neglects to touch a base.

EVALUATIVE CHECK LIST

1. Is each child developing skill in throwing and catching different kinds of balls?

2. Does each child know how to make a long, hard throw?

   a. Does he step forward on foot opposite throwing side?

   b. Does he get his hand moving as fast as possible before releasing the ball?

   c. Use the throwing arm as a "whip" pulling on the ball?

Three outs retire the batting team and the fielders become batters. Winner is the team with the most points after an equal number of innings have been played.

3. Is each player improving his ability to run the bases rapidly?

   a. Does he have the necessary endurance?

   b. Does he avoid slowing up or stopping for a base, thus losing momentum?

4. Do fielders work together to put runner out?

   a. Do they aim and throw carefully to basemen?

   b. Do they back up each other in case the ball is missed?

   c. Are they prepared to relay long throws from out-field to infield?

NOTES

Wall Pass

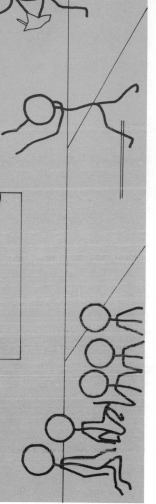

Players:
6–8 per group

Equipment:
basketball, wall target for each group; stopwatch

Behavioral goal: To throw a ball into a target as many times as possible in 30 seconds.

Mark several targets on a flat wall space, with six to eight children at each target. Target is a rectangle 8 feet wide and 4 feet high, at a distance of 3 feet from the floor. A restraining line is drawn on the floor 4 feet from the wall and parallel to the wall target.

Child number 1 in each group stands at any place in back of the restraining line. Child number 2 stands at the side where he can see the target easily and scores for number 1. Teacher uses a stopwatch to time all participants.

On signal "Go" child number 1 throws the basketball against the wall into the target, catching it as it rebounds, and continues throwing until the signal "Stop!" is given after 30 seconds. One point is given for each successful throw and his score is the total number of points.

If the ball gets out of control at any time, thrower must

recover it without assistance. A successful throw is one that goes into the target and is made from behind the restraining line. The ball may be caught on the fly or the bounce, as the thrower chooses. When the first child in each group has completed the test, the second child takes his place behind the restraining line and child number 3 scores for him. This continues until all children have been tested.

EVALUATIVE CHECK LIST

1. Is each child able to follow the testing directions accurately?
   a. Can he start and stop on signal?
   b. Can he throw from behind the restraining line?
   c. Does he stand in a forward stride position to aid balance and coordination?

2. Does each child understand how to improve his score?
   a. Does he catch balls on the fly rather than the bounce, if possible?
   b. Does he practice controlling hard, fast rebounds?

3. Does each child assume responsibility for scoring accurately when it is his turn to do so?
   a. Does he keep his eyes on the target?
   b. Does he keep accurate tally of successful hits?
   c. Does he start and stop scoring on the appropriate signal?

NOTES

Smorgasbord

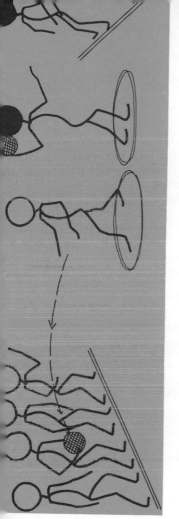

Players:
any number

Equipment:
basketballs

Behavioral goal: To pass and catch a basketball, using various types of pass.

Children divide into equal teams, 6–8 per team. The first player on each team stands inside a circle facing his team, whose members are lined up facing him. Each team member is assigned a specific type of pass before the game starts. For example:

Team member 1—chest pass
Team member 2—shoulder pass
Team member 3—bounce pass
Team member 4—overhead pass
Team member 5—underhand pass, using two hands
Team member 6—underhand pass, using one hand

On signal "Go!" the first player passes to each team member in turn, using his assigned type of pass. Team members use same type of pass in returning the ball. When ball reaches last player on team, that player runs with ball to circle and first player runs to head of line.

Throwing and Catching: grades 5, 6   251

Game continues until each player has had the circle position, and has passed to each team member in turn using the designated pass.

Winner is the team that first gets all players back to original positions.

EVALUATIVE CHECK LIST

1. Is each child able to perform the different types of passes, quickly and accurately?
   a. Does he step toward the person receiving his pass?
   b. Does he "give" as he catches the ball?
   c. Does he pass the ball immediately after catching it?

2. Are children considerate of each other?
   a. Do they avoid hard passes to less skilled players?
   b. Do they encourage each other?
   c. Do they give recognition to improved abilities?

3. Are children able to accept defeat without alibi or accusation?

4. Are children able to accept winning without boasting or ridicule?

NOTES

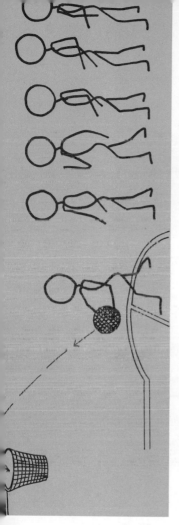

Players:
4–6 per group

Equipment:
basketball, goal

Behavioral goal: To practice shooting a basket successfully from different positions on the floor.

Each group has a basketball and a basket (goal). Each player in the group has a number and takes his turn in order. Each turn consists of three successive throws at the basket. The first throw is made from the free throw line and scores 5 points if successful. The next two throws are made from wherever the ball is recovered from the rebound. The second throw scores 3 points; the third throw, 1 point.

Game continues until one player reaches the exact score of 21. If player shoots more than 21 points, his score reverts to zero.

EVALUATIVE CHECK LIST

1. Is each child learning to shoot from different positions on the court?

2. Is each child learning how to perform various kinds of shot successfully?

3. Are children learning how to recover balls quickly on the rebound?

4. Does each child keep his score carefully and plan how to end up with exactly 21?

NOTES

of the Court

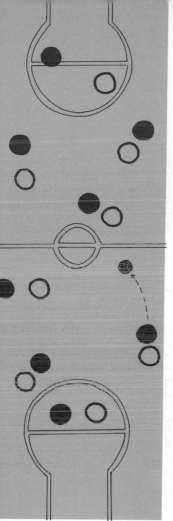

Players:
8 per team

Equipment:
basketball, court

Behavioral goal: To use passing, shooting, and guarding skills in playing the game; to win by helping one's team make the most points.

Children divide into two teams, eight players per team, with three forwards, three guards, one King of the Court, who does all of the shooting for the goal, and one Goal Defender. The game is played on a basketball court, each team playing on their own half. Forwards play on half court, guards play on opponents' court and guard opponents' forwards. King of the Court plays in his own free throw circle, and Goal Defender guards opponents'

King, playing also in the free throw circle of the opponents' court.

King is the only player who can shoot for basket and Defender is only player who can guard him and try to regain ball for his own team. King and Goal Defender are not permitted to move out of the free throw circle at any time and other players may not go into the free throw circle at any time.

In general, the rules of basketball govern fouls, penalties, and playing situations. The limited dribble may be used if desired, but this is primarily a passing game. The referee starts the game by throwing the ball to a forward, who receives it in the center circle and passes it to one of his team members. After each score, positions are rotated on the team making the score, with Goal Defender becoming King, Number 1 forward becoming Goal Defender, and King rotating to number 3 guard position, the last position in the rotation. A throw-in from the referee to a forward of the team *not* making score starts the game again.

Violations include (1) taking more than 1 step with ball in hands, (2) pushing, tripping, or roughing opponent, (3) playing in wrong playing area. Penalty for any violation: ball is awarded to opposing team. Each successful goal counts 2 points. Winner is the team with most points at end of playing time.

EVALUATIVE CHECK LIST

1. Does each child understand the rules of basketball?

2. Is each child improving his ball handling skills?

3. Is each child learning how to guard an opponent without fouling?

4. Are children good winners and losers?

NOTES

Forward Pass

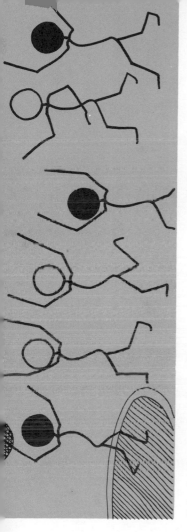

Players:
20–30

Equipment:
football

Behavioral goal: To pass a football over opponents' end line; to intercept opponents' passes.

Playing field is around 150 feet long, with two end lines and a center circle. Children divide into two teams. Ball is put into play by a team member standing in center of field, on center line, and passing to a teammate while opponents try to intercept the pass. Every completed pass gives the receiver the right to take three steps toward opponents' goal line before passing the ball. Every intercepted pass, whether touched, knocked down, or caught, causes the ball to be returned to the center line; the team intercepting the pass puts the ball into play.

A goal is made when the ball is passed over the opponents' end line and is not caught by opponents after it passes the end line. If ball is caught behind the goal line it is thrown back into field and is in play again.

EVALUATIVE CHECK LIST

1. Is each child able to pass and catch a football successfully?

2. Do team members plan how to cover their territory effectively?

  a. Do they intercept opponents' passes?

  b. Do they move ball directly toward goal?

3. Do team members assume responsibility for helping each other?

  a. Do they "back up" each other's catches?

  b. Do they encourage each other?

  c. Do they give less skillful players opportunities to handle the ball?

NOTES

Football

Players:
14–20

Equipment:
football or soccer ball

Behavioral goal: To advance the football over the opponents' line by passing, running, or kicking; to protect one's own goal line.

Children divide into two teams, with 7–10 players per team. One team starts the play by kicking or passing from their own half of the field with their backs toward their own goal. The ball may be advanced by means of a running play, a forward pass, or kicking. To start each play, the center must pass the ball backward to a teammate before any player may advance beyond the line of scrimmage, an imaginary line crossing the field from the spot where the center passes the ball.

In general, the rules of football govern fouls, penalties, and playing situations. Tackling is not permitted and "touching" is substituted for it. The ball carrier is touched or tagged on some part of his body below the neck. *Both hands must touch simultaneously.*

The size of the field, number of players, type of football used, and modification of rules should be governed by the ability and experience of the players. For elementary school children, a junior football or soccer ball may be used, and the field length should be roughly 60 yards. The game may be played in 5–8-minute quarters with rest periods between quarters. Players should wear rubber-soled tennis shoes and jerseys or pinnies to identify the teams easily. *No spiked shoes, shoulder pads, or helmets should be worn.*

For official football rules, write to the National Federation of State High School Athletic Associations, 7 South Dearborn St., Chicago, Illinois.

EVALUATIVE CHECK LIST

1. Does each child understand the rules of touch football? Does he understand:
   a. Fouls and penalties?
   b. Playing situations?

2. Is each child competent in the use of passing, kicking, and running skills?

3. Are team members able to cooperate in planning and executing plays to advance the ball toward the goal?
   a. Do they use team members' abilities to the best advantage?
   b. Do they use strategy in selecting the play to be used to advance the ball?

4. Do team members assume responsibility for helping each other?
   a. Do they back up each other's plays?
   b. Do they help less skillful players in practice sessions?
   c. Do they give all players opportunities to handle the ball in the game situation?

right hard. The weight is shifted forward to the left foot as the arm swings forward and strikes the ball. The follow-through permits the force of the movement to be absorbed by the extensors of the left knee and the rotators of the trunk. The recovery of balance is important, particularly if the child is expected to run immediately following the striking movement, as in the "sock ball" games. Striking the ball overhand is an extension of throwing, in that the ball is tossed up to oneself, lifted parallel to the body with the left hand and tossed about 18 inches above the head, slightly in front of the left shoulder. The right elbow leads the fist, as in throwing, until the ball is struck with the heel of the hand, which has made the fist. The shifting of weight and summation of forces are the same for striking the ball either overhand or underhand.

Batting is another form of striking; the arms are extended by the use of a bat, which gives a greater range of movement and consequently a greater application of force. The right-handed batter stands with his left side to the pitcher, weight balanced over both

STRIKING

Striking skills include (1) striking an object with the hand, (2) kicking an object, and (3) striking an object with an implement, such as a bat or paddle.

Striking a ball from an underhand position, as in serving a volleyball, consists of holding the ball in the left hand (for the right-handed striker); swinging the right arm back and then forward close to the

feet. He grips the bat with hands together, the right hand on top, and draws the bat back in readiness for the swing. As the ball is pitched, the batter steps toward the ball with his left foot and begins the weight shift. As the ball comes nearer, the batter rotates his trunk to the left, then the shoulder. This permits the bat to be pulled around in an arc, which is coordinated so that the heavy part of the bat comes in contact with the ball in front of the body. The batter's eyes remain on the ball until it is contacted by the bat. Good batting technique requires that the bat be swung in an arc parallel to the ground. This can be done if the left elbow is kept at approximately shoulder height and the end of the bat slightly higher until the ball is contacted. The weight of the bat should be such that the batter can easily hold it parallel to the ground with his arms extended.

Kicking is a skill widely used in many activities. There are basically two types of kick: (1) place-kicking, or kicking the ball from the ground, and (2) punting, or kicking the ball before it strikes the ground. Kicking the ball on the ground begins when the kicker is approximately one full step from the ball. The non-kicking foot is placed near the ball so that the kicking foot is in line with the ball. If the ball is struck above the center of mass it will result in a ground ball, and under the center of mass will result in air flight. Balance is maintained by slight knee flexion of the non-kicking leg, and the weight shift is followed by a backward lean.

In the punt, the ball is held in front of the body, weight is shifted to the kicking leg, and the body leans so that a preliminary step with the non-kicking leg will start the body moving in the direction of the intended kick. During the step the ball is raised to shoulder height and is released in a smooth drop, and the kicking leg is extended and swung forcefully into the ball as the body leans away from the ball. The ball is contacted with the top of the foot, not the toe. The timing of this sequence is critical, because a ball dropped too late will be kicked high and a ball dropped too early will be kicked low to the ground.

Striking skills are more complex than the running or throwing skills, and some children may find difficulty in mastering the coordination needed to contact

... g activities should be exploratory in nature, with balls of various types used by the child in many ways. Rubber balls may be bounced on the ground or may be batted into the air, but organized activities using these skills are not within the abilities and interests of this age group.

Kicking or striking a stationary target is less demanding than contacting a moving target, and the teacher may simplify games by substituting a stationary ball for a pitched ball when children are unable to contact the moving ball successfully. *For kindergarten chil-*

Kick Away

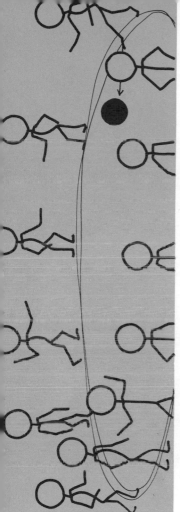

Players:
8–12 per group

Equipment:
one 8-inch rubber ball per group

Behavioral goal: To pass a ball across the circle, using inside of the foot.

Children stand around a circle. One player has ball on ground in front of him with his foot resting on it. Suddenly he says "Kick-away!" and kicks it across the circle, using the inside of his foot to avoid lofting it. The child receiving the ball kicks it quickly away from himself to another child. Children continue to kick ball until it goes outside of circle. The player who retrieves the ball brings it back to the circle and starts it again.

A large rubber ball should be used, and children should pass the ball to each other using the inside of the foot.

EVALUATIVE CHECK LIST

1. Is each child able to pass quickly, using the inside of the foot?

2. Is each child able to control the direction and force of his kick, even during the excitement of a game?

3. Does each child keep his position in the circle?

   a. Does he avoid kicking others?
   b. Does he kick only balls that come into his territory?

4. Are children considerate about kicking the ball to all parts of the circle, thus giving everyone a chance to kick the ball?

NOTES

Ball

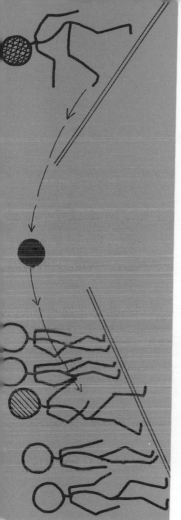

Players:
4–6 per group

Equipment:
one 8-inch rubber ball per group

Behavioral goal: To loft a rubber ball to the opposite line.

Two parallel lines are marked 30–40 feet apart. Child who is IT stands behind one line facing other players, who stand behind opposite line.

IT calls a player's name and lofts the ball toward the opposite line, using a punt or kicking the ball from the ground. Player whose name is called tries to catch ball and kicks it back to IT. This continues until IT has kicked it once to each player. Then IT calls "Free Ball!" and kicks toward the opposite line. Player who catches or stops the ball is the new IT.

Striking: grades 1, 2   267

EVALUATIVE CHECK LIST

1. Is each player able to kick the ball the necessary distance?

2. Is each child improving his ability to direct his kick toward a specific target?
   a. Does he move body toward direction of kick?
   b. Does he follow through by pointing foot in direction of kick?

3. Is each child learning how to catch or stop a hard-kicked ball?
   a. Does he move into position to catch the ball?
   b. Does he keep elbows and knees easy in catching?
   c. Does he give with the catch?

4. Do children help each other gain confidence in kicking and catching?
   a. Do they encourage each other to give their best effort?
   b. Do they avoid interfering with other players?
   c. Do they give suggestions for improvement when necessary?
   d. Do they avoid roughness or injury to others?

NOTES

the Wall

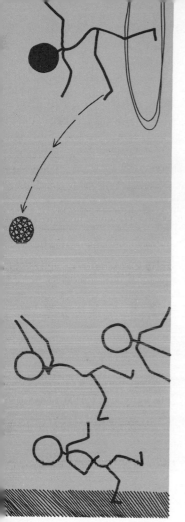

Players:
5–8 per group

Equipment:
one 8-inch rubber ball per group

Behavioral goal: To kick the ball "over the wall," to field the ball before it goes "over the wall."

The "wall" is a 25-foot line drawn a distance of 30–50 feet from the kicking circle. One player is the kicker and stands in the kicking circle. Other players scatter in playing field in front of wall.

Kicker places ball on ground inside kicking circle, calls "Over the wall!" and kicks toward the wall. Any fielder who can catch or stop the ball before it goes over the wall is the new kicker. If the ball crosses the line, or wall, the original kicker kicks again. If no one stops the ball after he has kicked three times, he chooses a new kicker.

If the ball goes out of bounds (over an imaginary line from the circle to each end of the wall), fielders call "Chase it yourself!" and run to the kicking circle. First fielder to reach circle is new kicker. Original kicker must chase his own out-of-bounds kick and return ball to new kicker.

EVALUATIVE CHECK LIST

1. Is each child able to kick the ball the necessary distance?

2. Is each child able to anticipate where the ball is going and move quickly to block or catch it?

3. Is each child able to catch a hard-kicked ball without injury?

   a. Does he trap the ball in hands and arms?

   b. Does he keep knees and elbows easy?

   c. Does he give with the catch?

4. Do children organize to avoid injury during "scramble" for ball by fielders?

   a. Do they avoid kicking ball from player in possession?

   b. Do they play in their own territory?

   c. Do they avoid collisions with other players?

NOTES

270

and Run

Players:
8–16 per group

Equipment:
one 8-inch rubber ball per group

Behavioral goal: To kick ball far enough to run around all four bases before it is retrieved.

Children divide into two teams, one in field and one at bat. First player on fielding team goes into field and first player on batting team places ball in kicking circle. When fielder is ready, kicker kicks ball into field and runs around bases and home. Fielder fields ball and runs directly to home base. When he reaches it he calls "Home!"

Kicker scores 1 point for each base he touches before fielder calls "Home!" For example, if kicker touches first

base only, he scores 1 point; if he runs past second base, he scores 2 points; and so on. After each player on the kicking team has had one turn at bat, the kickers become fielders and fielders become batters. Each player on fielding team has also had one turn in the field.

Individual scores may be kept, and winner is player with highest score, or a team score may be kept, winner being team with higher score.

EVALUATIVE CHECK LIST

1. Is each child able to kick the ball far enough to enable him to run one or more bases?

2. Does each child know how to improve his kicking?
   a. Does he move his body in direction of kick?
   b. Does he contact the ball underneath in order to loft it?
   c. Does he follow through with the kicking foot?

3. Does each child run bases efficiently?
   a. Does he start immediately after kick?
   b. Does he avoid stopping at each base, thus losing momentum?
   c. Does he continue running at full speed until after fielder calls "home?"

4. Do children encourage each other toward greatest effort?

NOTES

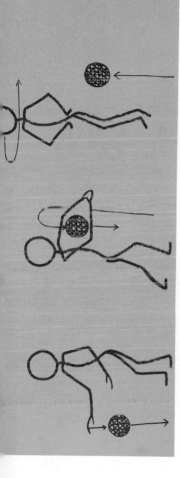

Players:
any number

Equipment:
1 rubber ball per player

Behavioral goal: To bounce a ball rhythmically to a chant while performing different stunts.

Game may be played as an individual activity, or small groups may chant and bounce balls together. Chant is as follows:

One and two and three O'Leary,
Four and five and six O'Leary,
Seven and eight and nine O'Leary,
Ten O'Leary Postman.

Player bounces ball on each accented word, then gives one hard bounce on "Postman" and catches the ball.

Suggested stunts to be done with the chant are as follows:

1. Bounce Ball on each accented word of chant, giving one hard bounce on "Postman" and catching ball in both hands.

2. Bounce ball as in (1), then make circle with arms on "O'Leary" and let ball drop through circle from above.

3. Bounce on accented words, then swing right (or left) leg over ball on "O'Leary."

4. Bounce, then turn all the way around on "O'Leary."

5. Make up your own stunt.

Striking: grades 1, 2   273

EVALUATIVE CHECK LIST

1. Does each child keep his eyes on the ball as he bounces?

2. Is each child able to determine the amount of force he needs to control the ball as it bounces?

3. Is each child able to bounce rhythmically to the chant?

4. Is each child able to perform the various stunts?

5. Is each child innovative in making up new stunts?

NOTES

Squares

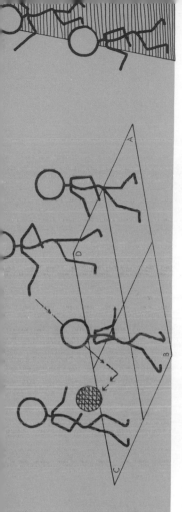

Players:
5 or 6 per group

Equipment:
one 8-inch rubber ball per group

Behavioral goal: To strike ball successfully into another player's square.

A court consisting of four squares is marked on a surface that will rebound a rubber ball. Each square is approximately 5 by 5 feet.

One child stands in each of the squares. The game starts when player D bounces the ball to any other player. The ball must land in the opponent's square and it must be played after the first bounce, with the receiving player bouncing it to any other player. The ball must bounce once in a square before it may be returned. The ball may not be held or caught.

Play continues until a player fouls.

A player fouls by:

1. *bouncing the ball on a line or out of the court;*
2. *hitting the ball with the fist;*
3. *holding the ball;*
4. *failing to return a ball that lands in one's square;*
5. *being hit by the ball—the player who is hit is down, not the server.*

Penalty for any foul is that the player who fouls goes

down to square *D* and other players move up in regular rotation from *D* to *C* to *B* to *A*. If the player in *D* fouls, he is out and goes to end of waiting line. Player at head of waiting line goes into *D*. Player in square *D* always starts the ball when play is resumed.

EVALUATIVE CHECK LIST

1. Is each child able to play the ball correctly?
   a. Does he wait until it bounces once in his square?
   b. Does he strike the ball with open palms into another player's square?
   c. Does he step toward the direction of movement as he strikes the ball?

2. Is each child alert and ready to strike the ball?

3. Does each child understand the rules of the game?
   a. Does he move to the appropriate position if he fouls?
   b. Does he start the ball in play when he is in *D*?

NOTES

Keep-Away

Players:
6–10 per group

Equipment:
1 soccer ball per group

Behavioral goal: To cooperate with team members in keeping the ball from the opposing team members.

Divide players into two teams. Team with ball tries to kick it in such a way that they pass it among themselves and keep it away from opposing team.

Players may not touch ball with hands, but must block it with the body. They may dribble by advancing the ball with short kicks, and trap or stop the ball with the feet. Ball should be passed with the inside of the foot rather than with the toe. Players may not kick, push, or rough each other.

EVALUATIVE CHECK LIST

1. Is each child improving his soccer skills?

   a. Does he pass soccer ball by contacting it below its center with inside of foot, following through across body in direction ball is passed?

   b. Does he dribble soccer ball by running beside or behind the ball as he uses inside of foot to kick ball 8–10 inches ahead?

   c. Does he block soccer ball with knee, hip or shoulder?

   d. Does he trap soccer ball with foot by placing sole of foot on top of ball with heel pointing downward in back of ball?

2. Do players include all team members in the game by passing to them?

3. Are children careful to avoid injury to others?

   a. Do they avoid hard kicks at close range?

   b. Do they avoid kicking or roughing other players?

NOTES

Ball

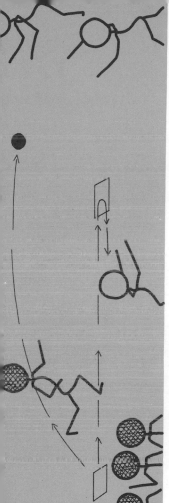

Players:
16–20 per group

Equipment:
one 8-inch rubber ball, home base
and first base

Behavioral goal: To strike the ball and run from home to first base and back without being put out.

Players divide into two teams, one team in the field and one at bat. Two bases are used, a home base and a first base. Fielders spread out in field, with one person playing baseman. First player of team at bat strikes the ball into the field with his hand and runs to first base and immediately back home. He may not stop on the base but must continue to home in one complete trip. If he makes the trip without being put out, he scores 1 run for his team.

Runner is out if:

1. a fielder catches a fly ball;
2. a fielder hits the runner below the waist with the ball before he reaches home; but fielders are not allowed to run with the ball in their hands.

When the team at bat makes three outs it goes into the field and the team in the field comes to bat. Winner is the team with most scores at end of playing period after an equal number of innings.

EVALUATIVE CHECK LIST

1. Is each child able to strike the ball successfully with his hand or fist?

   a. Does he hold ball in one hand and strike it with the other hand, stepping forward with foot opposite striking hand?

   b. Does he toss ball into air and strike it with his fist?

   c. Does he place the ball in the field in strategic position?

2. Are children improving in ability to throw a ball at a moving target?

   a. Do they throw in front of runner?

   b. Do they aim carefully below waist of runner?

3. Are children able to change direction quickly in running to first base and back to home?

   a. Do they touch first base, stop, and immediately push off in the opposite direction?

   b. Do they keep center of gravity low by bending knees, thus making a stronger push-off possible?

4. Do children cooperate in fielding the ball quickly and passing to teammates who are in good positions for hitting the runner?

NOTES

It
Up

Players:
any number

Equipment:
1 volleyball per team

Behavioral goal: To cooperate with teammates in keeping a volleyball in the air as long as possible.

Divide children into teams, five or six to a team. Each team has a volleyball. On signal "Go!" a team member tosses the ball into the air. Players keep striking it up into the air, using both hands. Team that keeps the ball up the longest wins 1 point. Team that makes most points at end of playing period is the winner.

Variation: If this game is difficult for the children, simplify it by permitting one bounce between each hit.

EVALUATIVE CHECK LIST

1. Is each child improving his skill in volleying the ball?
   a. Does he strike with both hands?
   b. Does he use pads of fingers rather than palms?

2. Do all team members participate in striking the ball?
   a. Do they pass ball from person to person?

   b. Are all players alert and ready to strike the ball when it comes to them?
   c. Do children try to play their own circle positions and avoid interfering with others?

3. Do players back each other up in case of a miss?

NOTES

Tag

Players:
10–15 per group

Equipment:
soccer ball

Behavioral goal: To kick a soccer ball at a moving target.

Boundaries of the playing area are determined and marked off. Players scatter within playing area. Three or four players are IT and they kick the soccer ball at the other players, trying to tag them below the knees with the ball. Anyone tagged by the ball is also It and helps tag others.

Kickers use inside of foot rather than toe to avoid lofting the ball. Kickers may also dribble ball with small, short kicks in an effort to get closer to other players.

Players may not touch ball with hands, but must block with body or feet. Game continues until all are tagged. Last player tagged is IT for next game and chooses other ITs to help him.

EVALUATIVE CHECK LIST

1. Is each child improving his soccer skills?
   a. Can he dribble with either foot or both feet?
   b. Can he pass accurately with inside of foot?
   c. Can he trap ball with foot?
   d. Can he block ball with body?

2. Do ITs cooperate to tag other players?
   a. Do they pass ball to each other when it would be advantageous to do so?
   b. Do they trap or block ball for each other?

3. Are children considerate of each other?
   a. Do they avoid roughness?
   b. Are they careful to aim below waist of runners?
   c. Do they avoid colliding with each other?
   d. Do they avoid hard kicks at close range?

NOTES

284

Old Cat

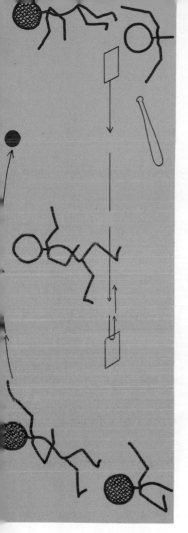

Players:
6–10 per group

Equipment:
softball, bat, 2 bases

Behavioral goal: To strike a ball successfully with a bat and run the bases without being put out.

Play area has a home plate and first base. Two of the players are batters and others are fielders numbered consecutively. Batters alternate catching position from one to the other.

Child at bat tosses ball into air and bats it into the field. There are no fouls, and all hits are good. When batter hits ball he must run to first base and home in one trip without being put out. If he is successful he makes 1 point and continues batting after serving as catcher for second batter. If he is put out, he becomes last fielder; fielders rotate positions from last fielder consecutively to first fielder; and first fielder becomes batter.

Batter is out if he:

1. *has three strikes at the ball and misses all three times;*
2. *is tagged while running (fielder with the ball tagging him);*
3. *does not reach home plate before catcher tags home with ball;*

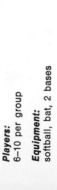

4. *hits a fly ball that is caught;*
5. *fails to touch bases while running;*
6. *throws his bat, rather than dropping it.*

EVALUATIVE CHECK LIST

1. Are children improving their batting skills?
   a. Do they toss ball out in front of them?
   b. Do they bat parallel to the ground when striking ball?
   c. Do they try to place ball in different parts of field?

2. Are fielders learning to catch hard-hit balls?
   a. Do they estimate where ball will land?
   b. Do they give with the ball when catching it?

NOTES

Any size rubber ball may be used while children are learning to bat. After children are successful in striking rubber balls, a spongy softball may be substituted.

3. Do fielders take stock of the situation and throw ball to most strategic position to get runner out?

4. Do base runners change direction quickly when moving from first base to home?
   a. Do they keep knees bent to lower center of gravity when stopping quickly?
   b. Do they push off strongly in direction of movement?

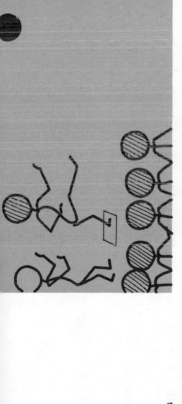

Base Kick Ball

Players:
12–20 per group

Equipment:
soccer ball, 2 bases

Behavioral goal: To punt a fair ball and score a home run.

Children are divided into two teams, one at bat and the other in the field. Playing field has a home base and a long base, which is approximately 30–40 feet from home base.

First player of team at bat stands behind home base and punts soccer ball (or football) into field. Then he tries to run to long base and home before fielders can throw the ball to the catcher. If he succeeds, he makes 1 run for his team.

Kicker does not score if:

1. *ball is returned to catcher before kicker gets home;*
2. *fly ball is caught;*
3. *kicker does not kick a fair ball in three trials—a "fair" ball must be punted and must land within agreed-upon boundaries.*

Batters stay at bat until each player has had a turn at

Striking: grades 3, 4 287

bat. Then batters become fielders and fielders become batters. Winner is team with higher score after even number of times at bat.

Variation: Game may be played with a pitcher, catcher, baseman, and fielders, and a softball and bat may be used in place of a soccer or football. Batter is out if he (1) strikes out, (2) bats a fly ball that is caught, (3) is tagged off base by a fielder with the ball, (4) reaches long base after baseman tags base with ball, (5) throws his bat. In this game, runners may be allowed to remain on long base if it is not safe to return home, and any number of runners may be on long base at same time.

EVALUATIVE CHECK LIST

1. Are children improving their punting skills?
   a. Is the ball held in front of body?
   b. Do they step forward on non-kicking leg and raise the ball to shoulder height?
   c. Do they drop ball, and swing forcefully with kicking leg, contacting ball with top of foot?

2. Do fielders wait in "ready" position, feet astride, knees flexed?

3. Are children learning how to catch hard-kicked balls?
   a. Do they anticipate where ball will land?
   b. Do they keep knees and elbows flexed?
   c. Do they give with the ball when catching it?

4. Are children able to respond accurately to all game situations as they arise?
   a. Do they back up each other's catches?
   b. Do they throw ball to most strategic place to get runner out?

NOTES

Net Ball

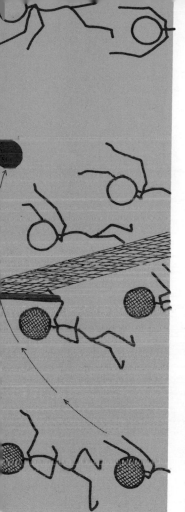

Players:
12–16 per group

Equipment:
volleyball, volleyball court, net

Behavioral goal: To strike a volleyball over the net successfully.

Divide children into two teams, each team on its own court on either side of net. Volleyball court should be about 25 by 50 feet, with top of net about 5 feet from ground.

Each team scatters on own side of net. Volleyball is given to one player, and on signal "Go!" he tosses it into air and hits it with both hands over net into opponents' court. Ball must bounce once in opponents' court and then must be hit over net before it bounces again. Any number of players may hit ball any number of times.

When ball bounces more than once in a court after crossing the net, it is one point for the opposing team. Team which loses the point starts the ball in play again. Fouls are:

1. *ball bouncing more than once in court;*
2. *ball thrown rather than batted;*
3. *ball caught and held;*
4. *ball hit with fist;*
5. *out-of-bounds ball.*

Penalties for all fouls: 1 point awarded to opposing team. Play is started again on side where foul occurred.

Winner is team with most points at end of playing period.

EVALUATIVE CHECK LIST

1. Are children improving skills needed for the game?
   a. Do they volley ball with both hands, using pads of fingers?
   b. Do they play the ball from a bounce without holding it?
   c. Do they set up ball for themselves or other teammates?

2. Do players decide upon positions on court?

   a. Do they play their own positions?
   b. Do they avoid interfering with teammates?
   c. Do they "back up" plays for teammates?

3. Does each child understand the rules of the game?
   a. Do they understand fouls and penalties?
   b. Do they use strategy in placing ball over net?

NOTES

and
Catch

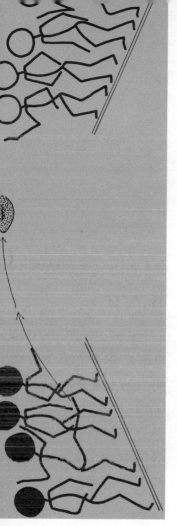

Players:
8–12 per group

Equipment:
soccer or football

Behavioral goal: To punt a ball over opponents' goal line; to field punted balls successfully.

Divide children into two teams, each team on its own goal line. Goal lines are 30–60 feet apart, depending upon the skill of the players. Team members number off and take turns punting in order.

Number 1 player on one team punts ball from own goal line over opponents' goal line. Any member of opponents' team may try to catch the ball. If the ball is caught on the fly, there is no score. If ball touches the ground before it is stopped, the kicker's team gets 1 point.

If the ball does not go over the goal line and receivers on opponents' team can catch it on the fly, one point goes to the receiver's team. Ball alternates from team to team until each player has punted. Team with most punts is the winner.

If most balls are falling short of goal, shorten distance between goals; lengthen the distance if most children are able to punt well beyond the goal line.

Striking: grades 5, 6   291

EVALUATIVE CHECK LIST

1. Is each child able to punt the necessary distance?

2. Does each child know how to improve his skill in punting?

   a. Does he hold ball in front of body?

   b. Does he step forward on non-kicking leg and raise ball to shoulder height?

   c. Does he drop ball and swing forcefully with kicking leg, contacting ball with top of foot?

3. Is each player improving his skill in catching a punted football?

   a. Does he anticipate where the ball will land and get in position for it?

   b. Does he keep knees and elbows easy?

   c. Does he give when the ball hits the hands?

4. Do team members work together cooperatively?

   a. Do they decide on an area for each player to cover?

   b. Do they play own positions and avoid interfering with other players?

   c. Do they back up each other's play in case of error?

NOTES

Players:
6–8 per group

Equipment:
softball, bat

Behavioral goal: To bat a ball successfully into the field; to field a grounder or fly ball successfully.

One player is batter and others are fielders. Batter tosses up ball and bats fly balls or grounders out into field. If a fielder can catch a fly ball or stop a grounder, he becomes batter and batter becomes fielder.

If no fielder succeeds in catching or stopping ball, first player to pick up the ball calls "Fungo!" Then batter lays bat on ground parallel to the fielder, who tries to roll ball over bat. If ball hits or jumps over bat, fielder who rolled the ball becomes batter. If ball misses bat, same batter continues batting.

EVALUATIVE CHECK LIST

1. Is each child able to toss ball into air and strike it into field?
   a. Does he toss ball out in front so end of bat can contact it?
   b. Does he strike ball with bat parallel to ground?

2. Is each child improving in ability to "place" balls by batting them to different positions in the field?

3. Does each child know how to stop hard-hit balls correctly?

   a. Does he anticipate where ball will be and move into position for it?
   b. Does he keep knees and elbows easy?
   c. Does he give with the catch?

4. Do children help each other if needed?
   a. Do they help player analyze his problems?
   b. Do they give suggestions for improvement?

NOTES

Ball

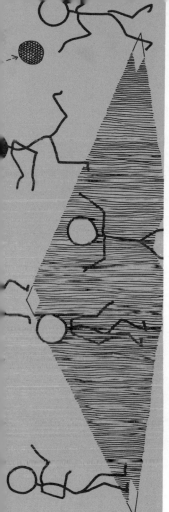

Players:
16–20 per group

Equipment:
soccer ball, 4 bases

Behavioral goal: To kick ball into field and circle bases before fielders relay ball to a base.

Players divide into two teams, one in field and the other at bat. Softball diamond is used, with bases 30 feet apart. Fielders take regular softball positions.

Pitcher rolls ball to batter, who kicks it into field and tries to circle bases before fielders relay ball. If ball beats runner around the bases, the runner is out. If runner beats ball, he scores 1 point for his team.

When ball is fielded, it must be thrown in order to first baseman, second, third, and home. Each baseman must

have one foot touching the base when he throws the ball to the next baseman. Batter is out if:

1. *fly ball is caught;*
2. *ball beats him around the bases;*
3. *he does not touch all bases as he rounds them;*
4. *he kicks four fouls.*

Three outs retire the side and fielders become batters. Winner is team with most points at end of playing period.

EVALUATIVE CHECK LIST

1. Is each child improving his skill in kicking a rolling ball?

2. Can fielders estimate where ball will land and move into position to catch it?

3. Do batters know and remember their batting order?

4. Do fielders work as a team?
   a. Do they relay ball quickly from outfield?
   b. Do they back up basemen in case they fumble the ball?
   c. Do they cover their positions?

5. Are basemen improving skills of passing and catching accurately under pressure?

6. Are players learning to play all positions?
   a. Do they see that everyone has a turn to play each position?
   b. Do they help weaker players when necessary?

NOTES

Choice

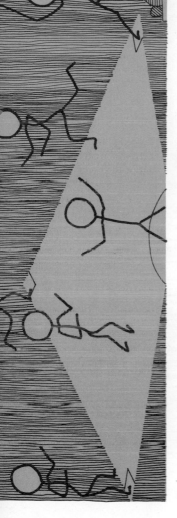

Players:
14–20 per group

Equipment:
different types and sizes of balls to be kicked, 4 bases

Behavioral goal: To kick a ball and run the bases without being put out.

Children divide into two teams, one at bat and the other in the field. Fielders play regular softball positions. A box of different types of balls that can be kicked, such as a football, a soccer ball, and different sizes of rubber utility balls, is placed back of home plate. The kicker chooses any ball he wishes and any type of kick he wishes and kicks it into the field, then runs bases consecutively from first to home without stopping on any base. If he gets home safely he scores 1 point for his team.

Kickers are out if:

1. *fielder catches a fly ball;*
2. *fielder throws the ball to a baseman before the runner reaches the base, with ball being passed in order from first to second, third, home and each baseman having one foot on the base as he throws to the next baseman;*
3. *kicker kicks three foul balls;*
4. *base runner neglects to touch a base.*

Three outs retire the kicking team, and the fielding team comes to bat. Winner is team with most points after an even number of times at bat.

EVALUATIVE CHECK LIST

1. Do fielders plan how to cover field space adequately?

2. Does each fielder play his own position?

3. Do fielders cooperate with each other to get runner out?

   a. Do they pass quickly to first baseman?
   b. Do they back up each other's catches?

4. Can players respond quickly to changing situations?
   a. Do they move quickly from kicking to base running?
   b. Do they move quickly from catching to throwing?

5. Are children improving in their abilities to punt or place-kick many different types of balls?

NOTES

Ball

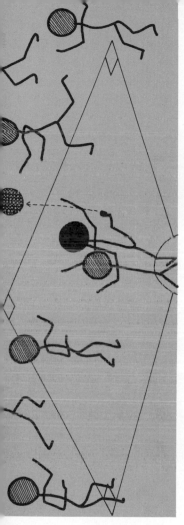

Players:
16–20 per group

Equipment:
soccer ball, 4 bases

Behavioral goal: To kick, run, and field successfully, using rules of the game of softball.

This game is played with two teams, using a softball diamond and softball rules. A soccer ball is used in place of the softball, with the pitcher rolling the soccer ball to the batter, who kicks it into the field.

Batter is out if he:

1. *strikes out by missing three balls that roll over home plate;*
2. *kicks four fouls;*
3. *kicks a fly ball that is caught;*
4. *is thrown out before he reaches base;*
5. *is tagged or thrown out before he returns to a base;*
6. *"leads off" a base;*
7. *steals a base except on an overthrow.*

Three outs retire the side, and the fielders come to bat. Winner is team with higher score after an even number of innings.

EVALUATIVE CHECK LIST

1. Is each child able to kick a rolling ball and place it in different positions in the field?

2. Do batters strategically place kicks so other base runners are able to score?

3. Are fielders able to decide quickly where ball is to be thrown?

4. Does each base runner know when to stay on base and when to move from the base?

5. Are children learning the rules of softball?

6. Do children have opportunities to play all positions at some time?

7. Do children willingly take turns in playing less favored positions?

NOTES

One
Bounce
Volleyball

Players:
12–16 per group

Equipment:
volleyball, volleyball court

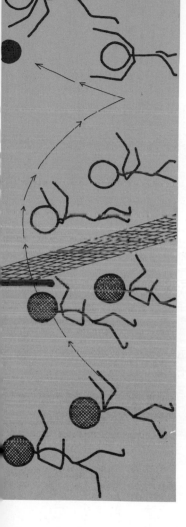

Behavioral goal: To strike a volleyball over the net successfully.

Players divide into two teams, one team on either side of the net. The volleyball court is about 25 by 50 feet, with top of net 6½ feet from ground. First player on serving team serves ball from behind serving line into opposite court. Server has two trials to make a good serve. If he succeeds, he serves until he fails to make a good serve, or until his team fails to return the ball to the opponents. Then the side is out and the opponents serve. The team scores 1 point for each successful serve

that opponents fail to return. After the side is out, players rotate positions for new server.

Each time ball crosses net it must bounce once in the court before it is returned. No player may hit a ball more than twice in succession, but any number of players may hit the ball. Fouls are:

1. *failure to make a good serve in two trials;*
2. *striking ball on return before it has bounced once;*

3. *allowing ball to bounce more than once;*

4. *player hitting ball more than twice in succession;*

5. *hitting ball with fist;*

6. *failure to return ball over the net;*

7. *out-of-bounds ball.*

Penalties for fouls:

1. *If serving team fouls, side out is called and the ball goes to the opponents.*

2. *If the receiving team fouls, 1 point is awarded to the serving team and the same server continues.*

The winning team is the one with the most points at end of playing period, (or the team that first reaches 21 points).

EVALUATIVE CHECK LIST

1. Is each child able to serve the volleyball successfully?
   a. Does he hold the ball in non-striking hand?
   b. Does he swing the striking arm back and then forward close to body?
   c. Does he contact the ball with heel of striking hand?
   d. Does he keep eyes on ball until contact?
   e. Does he step toward net with foot opposite striking hand as ball is struck?
   f. Does he place ball over net within boundaries?

2. Is each player learning how to "place" his serve in many different positions in opponents' court?

3. Are players improving in ability to volley the ball over the net?
   a. Do they strike ball with both hands?
   b. Do they strike with pads of fingers, rather than palms or fists?

4. Do children cooperate with teammates in playing the ball?
   a. Do they play own positions?
   b. Do they back each other up in case of error?

Newcomb

Players:
12–16 per group

Equipment:
volleyball, volleyball court

Behavioral goal: To volley a ball successfully in a game situation.

Players divide into two teams, one on either side of the net. The volleyball court should be about 25 by 50 feet, with net 6½ feet from ground. Ball goes to a player on one team, who tosses it into air and strikes it over net, using both hands. Opponents try to hit ball back over the net. The game continues until the ball strikes the ground in one court, which gives 1 point to the opponents. The ball is started again on the side where it hit the ground. Any player on the team may start the ball by tossing it into the air and striking it with both hands. There is no rotation or serving order. Any number of players may hit the ball any number of times. The fouls are:

1. *ball caught and held;*
2. *ball hit with fist;*
3. *ball thrown rather than batted;*
4. *out-of-bounds ball.*

Penalties for all fouls are 1 point awarded to the opponents. Play is started again on the side where the foul occurred. At the end of a certain length of playing time, the winner is the team with the most points.

EVALUATIVE CHECK LIST

1. Do children recognize that the purpose of the game is to give practice in volleying?

   a. Is each child able to volley correctly, using pads of fingers?

   b. Is each child able to control the ball and place it accurately in the opponents' court?

   c. Does each child play his own position, making it possible for all players to get practice in contacting the ball?

2. Do skillful players help less skillful teammates succeed?

   a. Do they volley ball to them frequently rather than always striking it over the net themselves?

   b. Do they practice volleying with them outside of the game situation?

NOTES

Badminton

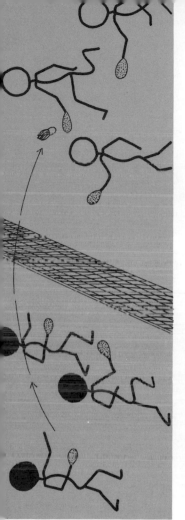

Players:
2–12 per group

Equipment:
long-handled paddles, shuttlecock or
fleece ball, net

Behavioral goal: To serve and volley a shuttlecock with a paddle.

Players divide into two teams, each team on its own
side of the volleyball court, with the top of net about
5 feet from the ground. First player on serving team
serves shuttlecock while standing behind the service
line. One service is allowed (with the exception of a
"let" bird, which is re-served. A "let" bird is one that
touches top of net as it goes over.) Serve must be
underhand. Any stroke may be used to return the
shuttlecock. It may not be hit twice in succession by
the same player, but any number of players may hit

it. A shuttlecock landing on boundary line is good.

Scoring is same as for volleyball. If receiving side
fails to return shuttlecock legally, 1 point is given to
serving side and server continues to serve. If serving
side fails, it is side out, and opponents serve. After side
out, players rotate (see arrows in picture) and new
server serves.

Two 10-minute halves are played, and team with
higher score is winner.

EVALUATIVE CHECK LIST

1. Are children able to serve shuttlecock successfully?
   a. Do they hold shuttlecock by the feathers with non-serving hand?
   b. Do they swing paddle back and then forward, using underhand serve?
   c. Do they drop shuttlecock at arms' length in front of body as paddle strikes it?

2. Does each child know area he is to cover and play his own position?

3. Do children use paddles safely?
   a. Do they swing paddles only when striking shuttle-cock?
   b. Do they avoid hitting other players?

4. Do children concentrate on keeping eyes on shuttle-cock until after striking it?

NOTES

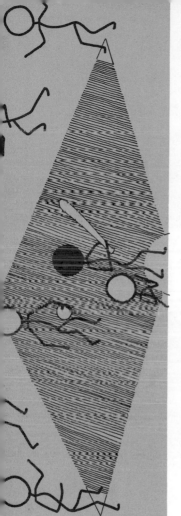

Players:
18–20 per group

Equipment:
softball, bat, 4 bases

Behavioral goal: To use batting, pitching, catching, fielding and running skills in the game of baseball.

Players divide into two teams, one at bat and the other in the field. Play area is a softball diamond with bases 45 feet apart. The pitcher throws the ball to the batter, using an underhand pitch. Batter tries to score a run by hitting a fair ball and running the bases from first to home in succession. He may stop on any base, but only one runner may occupy a base at one time, and runners may not pass each other. The batter is out if he:

1. *has three strikes;*

2. *is tagged or thrown out before reaching first base;*
3. *hits a fly ball that is caught;*
4. *throws the bat (optional).*

The base runner is out if he:

1. *is tagged by a fielder with the ball when off a base;*
2. *is forced to run, and the fielder with the ball reaches the base ahead of him;*
3. *runs from a base before a fly ball is caught, and is tagged*

Striking: grades 5, 6   307

before he returns to the base, or a fielder with the ball gets to the base before he returns;

4. leaves a base before the ball leaves the pitcher's hands;

5. fails to touch a base while running, or passes another base runner.

EVALUATIVE CHECK LIST

1. Is each child learning how to use the skills needed for playing the game?
   a. Does he bat a pitched ball successfully?
   b. Does he pitch an underhand ball?
   c. Does he catch a pitched or thrown ball?
   d. Does he throw a ball overhand from the field?
   e. Does he run the bases efficiently?

2. Do team members see that all players have a turn at playing favored positions?

After three outs, the batting team exchanges places with the fielding team. After both teams have been at bat an equal number of times, the team with the higher score is the winner (a regular baseball game has nine innings).

3. Do players courteously accept limitations of each member?
   a. Do they help each other to succeed?
   b. Do they encourage each other?

4. Are children learning strategy in playing the game?
   a. Do they set batting order with good hitters where they are most effective?
   b. Do they field ball and throw to bases where outs can be made most strategically to keep opponents from scoring?

NOTES

Back

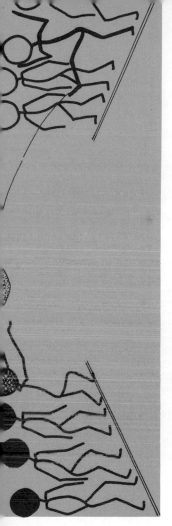

Players:
8–12 per game

Equipment:
football

Behavioral goal: To punt and catch a football.

Players divide into two teams. Each team has its own goal line approximately 250 feet from opponents' goal. Ball is given to one player who punts from his own goal toward opponents' goal. Other players on the punter's team stand behind own goal line.

Any player on the opposing team may receive the kick. The player who receives the ball punts from the point where he gained possession of it, with other members of his team scattered behind him. If the ball is caught on the fly, the player catching it may take two "giant" steps toward the opponents' goal before punting. If the ball is punted over the opponents' goal line and is not caught on the fly, the punter scores 1 point. If the ball is caught on the fly, there is no score, the ball is returned to the goal line, and the player who caught the ball punts from his own goal line toward the opponents' line. Out-of-bounds balls are punted from side line at point where they went out.

The winner is the team with the most points at the end of a given playing period.

EVALUATIVE CHECK LIST

1. Is each child able to punt a football correctly?
   a. Does he shift weight to kicking leg and lean so that a step with non-kicking leg will start the body moving in the direction of the kick?
   b. Does he raise ball to shoulder height during step and release it smoothly in line with kicking leg?
   c. Does he keep non-kicking leg planted and kicking leg extended, and swing it forcefully into the ball as the body leans away from the ball?
   d. Does he contact ball with top of foot, not toes?

2. Is child able to catch a football effectively?

   a. Does he stay in line with oncoming ball?
   b. Does he relax body and keep eyes on ball?
   c. Are hands and fingers relaxed; do arms and body give with impact?

3. Do players make it possible for all team members to participate?
   a. Do they take turns receiving the ball?
   b. Do they back up the receiver?

4. Are children able to analyze punts and plan how to improve each punt?

NOTES

interesting games from home to share with the class, and creativity in developing new games is also desirable.

Other types of activities suitable for the classroom are singing games and folk games. Pocket guides that present a good selection of these activities are:

KRAUS, RICHARD, *A Pocket Guide of Folk and Square Dances and Singing Games for the Elementary School* (Englewood Cliffs, N. J.: Prentice-Hall, Inc., 1966).

LATCHAW, MARJORIE and JEAN PYATT, *A Pocket Guide of Dance Activities* (Englewood Cliffs, N. J.: Prentice Hall, Inc., 1953).

CLASSROOM GAMES

Classroom games are useful when inclement weather prohibits outdoor activity, or when children need a recreational break in the regular program to relieve tension or fatigue. Classroom games are also fun for special occasions and lend a "party" atmosphere to holidays.

The games included in this selection may be played in the typical classroom setting and use simple

Tommy Tiddlemouse

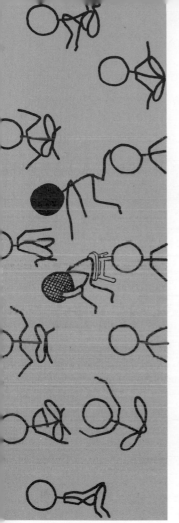

Players:
any number

Equipment:
none

Behavioral goal: To guess who is knocking on one's "house."

Children sit in large circle in center of room. One child, who is Tommy Tiddlemouse, sits on a chair in center of circle and hides his eyes. Teacher points to or touches a child in the circle. Child moves quietly toward Tommy's chair as children chant:

Little Tommy Tiddlemouse lives in a little house,
Someone is knocking, oh me! oh my!
Someone is calling, "It is I!"

Child who was indicated by teacher knocks on Tommy's chair and says, "It is I," at appropriate places in rhyme, and Tommy tries to guess the child from his voice. If he guesses correctly in three guesses, everyone claps for him. In any event, a new Tommy is chosen by the old one and the game continues.

Variation: The game "Doggie, Your Bone Is Missing" is similar, with child in center the "doggie"; a "bone" (eraser or other object) is placed under his chair. A child indicated by the teacher quietly takes the bone, returns to his place in the circle, and hides it in back of him. Children say, "Doggie, your bone is missing," and the "doggie" tries to guess who has it.

EVALUATIVE CHECK LIST

1. Is each child able to carry out his own game responsibility?
   a. Does Tommy keep eyes closed and not peek?
   b. Do children chant together, stopping on "It is I"?
   c. Does the child knock and speak at appropriate places in rhyme?

2. Does Tommy choose a child who has not had an opportunity to be IT for the new Tommy?

3. Are children gradually assuming more responsibility for conducting the game?
   a. Can a child take teacher's role of touching someone in the circle?
   b. Can children choose new Tommys and new "teachers" without help?
   c. Can each child carry out his own game responsibility without coaching?

NOTES

Hunt

Players:
any number

Equipment:
none

Behavioral goal: To mimic the action of a story; to make up a story for others.

Children sit in seats or on floor facing teacher. Teacher tells a story about a lion hunt, making rhythmic motions illustrating the action. The children follow the motions of the teacher. The teacher may tell a favorite story, or may be as creative as he wishes in making up a story. If he wishes, he may have children participate in telling the story by asking a child to tell and show what happened next. Here is an example of a story about a "lion hunt":

I was walking slowly through the jungle one day (*slap hands alternately on knees, simulating a slow walk*) looking for a lion (*form binoculars with hands and put to eyes*). I came to a river and had to swim across (*swimming motions*) and when I got to the other side, I shook the water from my body (*shake*).

Suddenly, I heard a lion roar, so I quickly climbed a tree (*climbing motions*) and looked all around for the lion (*binoculars*). I saw a lion sitting on a hill,

swam to the other side (*fast swimming*), shook off the water (*shake quickly*), and ran through the jungle all the way home (*running motions with hands on knees*). And that was the end of my lion hunt.

licking his whiskers (*lick whiskers*), so I decided I had better go home. I climbed quietly down the tree (*climb down*), tiptoed toward the river (*fingers imitate tiptoe on knee*), when the lion saw me and gave a great roar. I dived into the river (*hands together, as if diving*),

EVALUATIVE CHECK LIST

1. Are children able to follow plot and action of the story?

   a. Do they mimic the movement at the appropriate time?

   b. Are they able to participate in telling the story and showing the action?

2. Does each leader continue each movement long enough for each child to feel the rhythm and respond with the group?

3. Are the children becoming increasingly creative in helping the teacher think of ideas for stories and appropriate actions?

   a. Do they use seasonal ideas, such as *Halloween Night*, or *Christmas Eve in the Toy Store*?

   b. Do they use ideas related to the world around them, such as *A Visit to the Park*, or *A Trip to the Moon*?

   c. Do they use ideas related to occupations, transportation, animals, and the like?

   d. Do they use ideas related to favorite books, television characters, sports heroes, and the like?

   e. Other?

NOTES

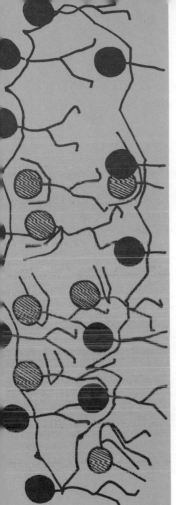

Players:
any number

Equipment:
none

Behavioral goal: To be the last "mouse" caught in the "trap."

Half the children stand in a circle with hands joined to form the "trap." The trap is open when joined hands are raised over heads, and trap is shut when joined hands are lowered to sides.

Other children are "mice." Game starts when teacher says, "Trap open!" Circle players raise joined hands and the mice weave in and out through the trap. When teacher says, "Snap!" the trap closes and all mice inside the circle are caught. Mice who are caught join the circle and become trap. Game continues until all mice are caught. Then original mice become trap and players who formed the original trap become mice.

If any mice try to break out of the circle when the trap closes, they are considered caught and join the trap.

Variation: A similar game is "Butterflies and Daisies." Half of players are "daisies" and squat on floor as in a flower bed; others are "butterflies," and when music starts they flit about among the daisies. When music stops, butterflies freeze; daisies touch as many butterflies as they can reach from their sitting or squatting positions. These butterflies become daisies and sit in bed with other daisies. Game continues until all butterflies are caught; then original butterflies become daisies and vice versa as game is repeated.

EVALUATIVE CHECK LIST

1. Does trap open and close quickly on signal?

2. Do all mice move in and out of trap, rather than staying on the outside?

3. Do mice accept capture without complaint, and move quickly to join the circle?

4. Are children becoming increasingly competent in controlling the game themselves?
   a. Do they follow all rules without complaining?
   b. Do they take teacher's role of opening and closing trap?

NOTES

the Bridge

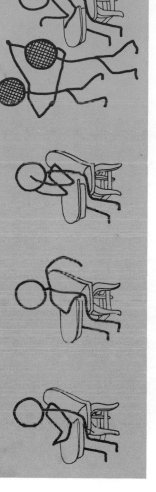

Players:
any number

Equipment:
piano or record

Behavioral goal: To move with another while the music plays, stopping when it stops and lowering the "bridge."

All children remain in seats except two children, who clasp hands to form a "bridge." Bridge stands on either side of a seat with hands clasped over the child. When the music starts, the bridge moves around the room with clasped hands passing over each child. When music stops, bridge stops moving and is lowered over the child who is under it. If bridge happens to be between two children at the time the music stops, it moves forward to the next child.

The child who is captured chooses a partner and both bridges move around the room passing over the seated children, when the music starts. Game continues until all have been bridges.

Variation: A similar game is the old folk game, "London Bridge Is Falling Down," in which two children form the bridge and other children pass under as all chant, "London bridge is falling down, falling down, falling down; London bridge is falling down, my fair lady." Bridge is lowered on "lady," and child who is trapped chooses to be on the side of either bridge member.

EVALUATIVE CHECK LIST

1. Is each child able to move and stop with another?
   a. Does he keep hands joined?
   b. Does he avoid pulling or jerking partner?
   c. Does he stop immediately when music stops?

2. Are children able to carry out game responsibilities?
   a. Do "bridge" players stay on either side of seated children, with clasped hands over children's heads?
   b. When music stops, do they lower "bridge" immediately?
   c. When seated, do they keep feet under chair to avoid tripping "bridges"?

NOTES

Buckle
Beanstalk

Players:
any number

Equipment:
object to hide

Behavioral goal: To find the hidden object before the other players see it

An object to be hidden is selected, such as a block, scarf, or eraser. One child is IT. After several children leave the room, IT hides the object in plain sight; that is, the children should be able to see it without opening or lifting anything.

Children who left the room are called back in and look for the object. Other children in room look in other directions to avoid giving its location away. As soon as a seeker sees the object, he goes quickly to his seat and says, "Huckle Buckle Beanstalk." Others

continue hunting until each one has seen it and has gone to his seat. Child who first saw the object is the new IT.

If children search too long, clues may be given to help them, such as clapping very loudly when they are "hot" and very softly when they are "cold."

Variation: A similar game is "I Spy." Children hide their eyes and IT hides the object in plain sight. Then children open their eyes and the first one to see the object says, "I spy," and becomes the new IT.

EVALUATIVE CHECK LIST

1. Is IT innovative in finding places to hide the object?

2. Do seekers search purposefully, rather than running about aimlessly?

3. Does child go quietly to his seat when he sees object, without giving its location away to other searchers?

4. Do children avoid giving clues by looking at the object?

NOTES

Come
With
Me

Players:
any number

Equipment:
none

Behavioral goal: To follow the leader, then run quickly to one's seat on signal.

One child is the leader. He walks around the room and touches a player on the shoulder, saying, "Come with me." Players who are touched by him follow him around the room.

After touching five or six players, he turns quickly and claps his hands over his head. Players run back to own seats. First child to reach his seat is the new leader. If so desired, there may be several leaders touching players, making it possible for more children to play at one time.

Variation: This game may also be seasonal. The leader may be Santa Claus selecting toys; when he says, "Merry Christmas," children run to their seats. A leader may be a witch and say "Hocus pocus" as a signal for players to run to their seats.

EVALUATIVE CHECK LIST

1. Does leader perform his role effectively?
   a. Does he select children quickly?
   b. Does he move children away from seats before giving signal to run?
   c. Does he choose children who have not been previously chosen?

2. Do children who are chosen react quickly to signal?

   a. Do they keep themselves aware of most direct route to seat?
   b. Are they ready to go on signal?

3. Do seated players cooperate with runners?
   a. Do they keep feet out of running territory?
   b. Do they avoid distracting the runners?

NOTES

Object Pass

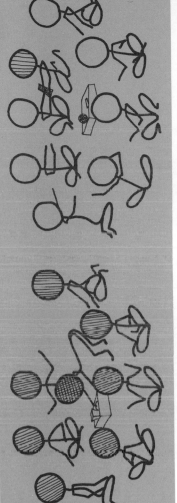

Players:
any number

Equipment:
3 objects per team

Behavioral goal: To work with teammates in quickly passing the ball over and under to the end of the line.

Children divide into two or more even teams. Each team sits in a circle or line, depending upon room space. In a central place in the room is placed a box for each team. Each box has three objects in it, such as beanbag, chalk, eraser, and the like.

On signal "Go!" the leader of each team runs to his box, takes out one object, carries it back to his team and passes it around the circle, or down the line. As soon as he has started the object on its way, he returns

to the box and gets the second object, starts it from player to player, and then gets the third. The player at the end of the circle or line puts the object back into the box as soon as he receives it. The team that first gets all objects back into the box is the winner.

Variations: Players may stand in file formation (one behind the other) and on signal, first player in line passes a beanbag or ball over his head to player in back of him; this player passes it through his legs to next player, who passes it over the head, and so on to end of line. Then line faces opposite direction and ball is passed back over and under to first player.

In another variation, the ball is passed over the head to the next player and when it reaches the end of the line, the last player in line runs to the front of the line with the ball and immediately passes it over his head to the player in back. This continues until the line is in the original position.

EVALUATIVE CHECK LIST

1. Are children able to handle objects of various sizes, shapes, and weights with speed and efficiency?

2. Is each child able to concentrate on the job at hand?
   a. Is he ready to receive and immediately pass an object?
   b. Does he control his excitement and avoid dropping the objects?

3. Do the first and last players in the line move quickly to the box at the appropriate times?

NOTES

Guard the Moon

Players:
any number

Equipment:
none

Behavioral goal: To guard the "moon" from invasion; to be one of the first three Earth Men to invade the moon.

The "moon" is a large circle about 8 feet in diameter, drawn on the floor in the front of the room. Three players are Moon Men and it is their function to protect the moon from invasion. The other children are Earth Men and are trying to invade the moon. On signal "Start!" children try to get on the moon without being tagged by the Moon Men.

Any child who is tagged before he places a foot on the moon must return to his seat and remain there until

the next game. If a child places his foot on the moon before being tagged, he is safe and remains inside the circle. When three children safely invade the moon, the game is over. The three invaders become the new Moon Men, and a new game is started with the signal.

Variations: In a similar game, "Classroom Tag," a line is drawn in the front of the room, one child is IT, and the teacher calls the names of three children, who must try to get across the line without being tagged by IT. If a player is tagged, he must return to his seat; last one to be tagged is new IT.

Another similar game is "Seat Tag," in which the child who is IT stands in front of room. Teacher calls names of two children who must change seats before being tagged by IT. If IT tags a child successfully he continues to be IT; if not, he chooses a new IT.

EVALUATIVE CHECK LIST

1. Do Moon Men cooperate in guarding the moon from the invaders?

   a. Do they guard assigned positions?

   b. Do they assist each other when necessary?

2. Do invaders try to use strategy in outmaneuvering the guards?

   a. Do they watch for an opening to slip through the guards?

   b. Do they force guards to move continually from one position to another?

3. Do children assume game responsibilities?

   a. Do they go to seats immediately if tagged?

   b. When seated, do they avoid interfering with runners?

   c. If safe on "moon," do they stay quietly without interfering with guards or other players?

NOTES

Eraser
Tag

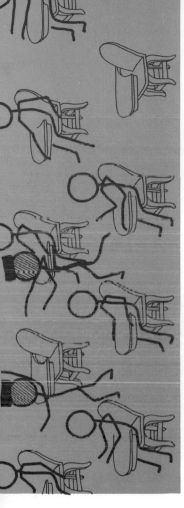

Players:
any number

Equipment:
2 chalkboard erasers

Behavioral goal: To successfully balance an eraser on one's head while chasing or fleeing.

One child is IT and places an eraser on his head, handing the other eraser to any seated player. This player places the eraser on his head and tries to tag IT before IT can save himself by getting into the chaser's seat. Neither player may touch his eraser at any time *after* putting it on his head. If either player loses his eraser (lets it drop off his head), the other person is the winner.

If IT can reach the seat safely without being tagged or losing his eraser, he is the winner. If the chaser does not lose his eraser and tags IT before IT reaches his seat, the chaser is the winner. The winner becomes the new IT, and the loser chooses a new chaser and gives him the eraser.

If there are many players, several ITs may play.

EVALUATIVE CHECK LIST

1. Does each child place the eraser carefully on his head before moving?

2. Is each child able to resist touching his eraser after it is on his head?

3. Is each child able to balance his eraser while moving quickly?

4. Do seated children cooperate with runners?
   a. Do they keep feet out of running area?
   b. Do they avoid touching or distracting runners?

NOTES

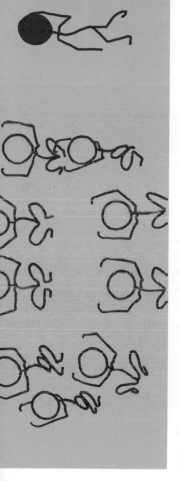

the
Leader

Players:
10–12 per group

Equipment:
none

Behavioral goal: When one is IT, to guess the person who is leader.

Children sit in a circle. One player is IT and leaves the room. A circle player is leader and starts a motion, such as swinging arms, tapping head, wiggling foot, or hunching shoulders; other players immediately follow his movement.

IT is called back into the room, and as the group follows the leader, changing from motion to motion, IT tries to guess which person is the leader. Players try to keep IT from knowing who is leader by looking at each other as they follow changes. Leader also tries to confuse IT by looking at another player as though he thought he were the leader.

If IT finds leader in three guesses, he may choose a new IT for the next game. If he is unsuccessful, the leader chooses a new IT. When new IT leaves the room, the old leader points to a new leader and the game continues.

EVALUATIVE CHECK LIST

1. Do children try to keep leader concealed from IT?
   a. Do they avoid looking directly at the leader?
   b. Do they quickly follow the movement changes?

2. Are leaders innovative in finding new and different movements?
   a. Do they experiment with all body parts?
   b. Do they change the movement frequently?

3. Does IT make his three guesses within a reasonable length of time?

4. Do children try to give everyone a chance to partici-pate?
   a. Do they choose new players to be IT?
   b. Do they choose new leaders who have not been IT?

NOTES

Magic

Players:
any number

Equipment:
none

Behavioral goal: To catch on to the trick of "black magic."

Two players are "in cahoots." One player is the Magician and leaves the room. His partner asks the group in the room to decide on some object, such as "Mary's desk." The Magician is called back into the room and his partner asks, "Is it the door?" The Magician answers "No," and continues to answer "No," to every question, until the question *after* the partner asks about something that is black in color. For example, the partner may ask, "Is it the blackboard?" and the Magician says "No," but he knows that the next question will be

the correct object. "Is it Mary's desk?" and the answer is "Yes."

Remember the clue: The object asked *after a black object* is mentioned is the right one. If the players catch on to the trick, confuse them by using a red-white-blue variation, asking first a red object, then a white, then a blue before the correct object. When a player thinks he is on to the trick, test him by letting him be the Magician.

Variation: Players use a "magic wand." Trick is

Classroom Games: grades 3, 4   333

that the partner with the wand points it toward some person in the room before the Magician leaves. The Magician knows that the partner will eventually point toward this person again, and the object he selects immediately afterward is the correct object. Player with wand may also point to different objects and ask, "Is it this?" or "Is is that?" mixing up his questions to confuse the audience.

EVALUATIVE CHECK LIST

1. Do players "in cahoots" understand their roles?
   a. Do they practice beforehand?
   b. Do they give players who are on to the trick a chance to be Magicians too?

2. Do children prepare other tricks to present to the class?
   a. Do they bring magic tricks from home?
   b. Do they look in game books to find new tricks, and practice before showing them to the class?

NOTES

Relay

Players:
any number

Equipment:
chalkboard, chalk

Behavioral goal: To cooperate with one's team in completing the drawing of the "cootie" before the other teams complete theirs.

Children divide into even teams, 8–10 per team. Team members sit facing chalkboard. On signal "Go!" first player in each line runs to board, draws some part of the "cootie" (see illustration), places chalk on board tray, and returns to his seat. When he is seated, next player in line goes. Team that finishes first is the winner.

The number of legs, eyes, or ears on cootie depends upon the number of players in each team. Group should decide before playing how finished cootie must look.

Variations: Other ideas may be used, such as jack-o-lanterns, objects from outer space, Christmas tree, valentine, and the like.

EVALUATIVE CHECK LIST

1. Does each child know how the finished picture should look?

2. Is each child able to quickly determine the part he should add to the drawing when it is his turn?

3. Do children encourage their teammates?

4. Are children innovative in thinking of other things to draw, such as:

   a. Life in an aquarium?
   b. Storybook character?
   c. Holiday representation?
   d. Transportation vehicle?
   e. Other?

NOTES

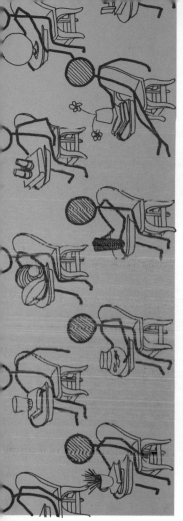

Hunt

Players:
any number

Equipment:
any available articles

Behavioral goal: To collect a given list of articles within the time period.

Children divide into teams, six to eight per team. Each team is given a list of articles to collect within a given time limit. Team that collects most articles is winner.

Articles may be related to a specific theme, such as social studies unit, science unit, or other class activity, or they may be any articles available in the classroom. Examples: yellow pencil or tablet; book with a picture of a dog; spelling paper with an A on it; red shoe; string, 2 inches long; book with the word "atomic" in first sentence of a paragraph; envelope with a stamp on it; signs of the zodiac, and the like.

EVALUATIVE CHECK LIST

1. Are children resourceful in finding the articles?

2. Does each child participate significantly in helping his team obtain the articles?

3. Are children becoming independent in playing this game without adult supervision?

a. Do they appoint a student committee to set up list of articles and organize the game?

b. Do they plan how to organize teams that are equal in ability, depending upon the theme of the game?

NOTES

338

Concentration

Players:
20 or more

Equipment:
available objects

Behavioral goal: To recall the order of the players and the objects each held.

Eight or 10 players line up in front of room, holding some object in front of them. Other players observe carefully for one minute. Players with objects leave room, in order. Observers try to write down order in which players were standing, and name the object each was holding.

Observers exchange papers, and players with objects return in correct order. Papers are checked, and winner is observer with most correct answers.

Variation: Place several objects on a table; players observe them for one minute. Objects are covered, and players write down as many as they can recall.

EVALUATIVE CHECK LIST

1. Does each observer concentrate on his task?
   a. Does he try to block out extraneous images?
   b. Does he try to attack the problem with confidence?

2. Do group members make it possible for each person to do his best?
   a. Do they avoid distracting others?
   b. Do they maintain silence until others have finished writing?

3. Are children accurate in checking each other's papers?

4. Are players with objects careful to maintain their positions in line?

NOTES

Third

Degree

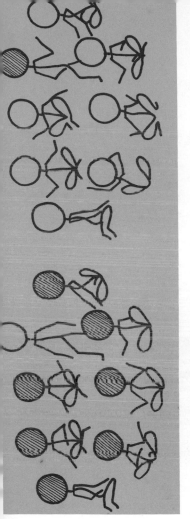

Players:
any number

Equipment:
none

Behavioral goal: To ask questions that make it possible to guess the object before the other teams guess it.

Children divide into teams, six to eight per team. Each team chooses a leader. Leaders meet together and agree on a specific object.

Each leader goes to a team other than his own. Team members try to identify the object by asking the leader questions, to which he must answer "Yes," "No," or "I don't know." Team that first guesses the object is the winner.

If desired, 1 point may be given to each winner and the team with the greatest number of points at the end of the playing period wins the game.

EVALUATIVE CHECK LIST

1. Do children first ask general questions to narrow the field of possibilities?

2. Does each child try to remember the answers?

3. Is each member of the group given equal opportunity to ask questions?

4. Are group members courteous to each other and to the visiting leader?

   a. Wait for questions to be completed and answered before asking another?

   b. Treat leader courteously at all times?

NOTES

INDEX